Cambridge Elements ≡

Elements in Publishing and Book Culture
edited by
Samantha Rayner
University College London
Rebecca Lyons
University of Bristol

ADAPTING BESTSELLERS

Fantasy, Franchise and the Afterlife of Storyworlds

Ken Gelder
University of Melbourne

CAMBRIDGE
UNIVERSITY PRESS

CAMBRIDGE
UNIVERSITY PRESS

University Printing House, Cambridge CB2 8BS, United Kingdom

One Liberty Plaza, 20th Floor, New York, NY 10006, USA

477 Williamstown Road, Port Melbourne, VIC 3207, Australia

314–321, 3rd Floor, Plot 3, Splendor Forum, Jasola District Centre,
New Delhi – 110025, India

79 Anson Road, #06–04/06, Singapore 079906

Cambridge University Press is part of the University of Cambridge.

It furthers the University's mission by disseminating knowledge in the pursuit of
education, learning, and research at the highest international levels of excellence.

www.cambridge.org
Information on this title: www.cambridge.org/9781108731089
DOI: 10.1017/9781108589604

First published 2019

A catalogue record for this publication is available from the British Library.

ISBN 978-1-108-73108-9 Paperback
ISSN 2514-8524 (online)
ISSN 2514-8516 (print)

Adapting Bestsellers

Fantasy, Franchise and the Afterlife of Storyworlds

Elements in Publishing and Book Culture

DOI: 10.1017/9781108589604

First published online: December 2019

Ken Gelder

University of Melbourne

Author for correspondence: Ken Gelder, kdgelder@unimelb.edu.au

ABSTRACT: This Element looks at adaptations of bestselling works of popular fiction to cinema, television, stage, radio, video games and other media platforms. It focuses on 'transmedia storytelling', building its case studies around the genre of modern fantasy, because the elaborate storyworlds produced by writers like J. R. R. Tolkien, J. K. Rowling and George R. R. Martin have readily lent themselves to adaptations across various media platforms. This has also made it possible for media entertainment corporations to invest in them over the long term, enabling the development of franchises through which their storyworlds are presented and marketed in new ways to new audiences.

KEYWORDS: fantasy, bestsellers, adaptation, franchise, storyworlds, transmedia storytelling

ISBNs: 9781108731089 (PB), 9781108589604 (OC)

ISSNs: 2514-8524 (online), 2514-8516 (print)

Contents

1 Introduction: Adaptation, Franchise
and Modern Fantasy   1

2 The Afterlife of Modern Fantasy   16

3 Adapting J. R. R. Tolkien   34

4 J. K. Rowling and the Potterverse   49

5 George R. R. Martin and HBO's *Game of Thrones*   63

References   77

1 Introduction: Adaptation, Franchise and Modern Fantasy

This book will look at adaptations of bestselling works of popular fiction to cinema, television, stage, radio, video games and other media platforms. It focuses on what is often called 'transmedia storytelling': 'the development of transmedia storytelling', as Mélanie Bourdaa has noted, 'implies that a story is complex enough to create and expand a whole coherent universe around it' (Bourdaa, 2013, pp. 202–3). The case studies in this book are built around the genre of modern fantasy, because the elaborate fictional worlds of modern fantasy have readily lent themselves to transmedia storytelling – that is, adaptations across various media platforms. The adaptation of literary works to other media platforms can radically amplify their range and impact. But fantasy writers such as J. R. R. Tolkien, J. K. Rowling and George R. R. Martin had in fact already begun to proliferate storyworlds as 'universes' (e.g., the 'Potterverse') in their own novels. Because their novels sold well early on and worked to develop a coherent narrative over an extended period of time – comprising a series, released in sequence one novel after the other – their storyworlds made it possible for media entertainment corporations to invest in them over the long term. For these three writers – and also for others in the modern fantasy genre – adaptations provided the 'pretense' (Meikle, 2019, p. 14) for the development of franchises through which their storyworlds could be promoted, distributed and marketed in new ways and to new audiences.

The often-complex process of adaptation to another media platform entails a number of negotiated adjustments involving narrative, plot, event, characters, casting, design, voice, sound and so on. Adaptation, to state the obvious, is transformative; the nature of the transformation depends on the creative, financial and technical properties and priorities of any given media platform. But in the case of some popular literary genres – like modern fantasy – adaptation also brings with it the potential for the corporate transformation of bestsellers into brands and franchises that can be merchandised across a range of cultural sectors. So transmedia storytelling can also become what Clare Parody has called 'franchise storytelling'. As she puts it, '[f]ranchise storytelling may be defined as the creation of narratives, characters and settings that can be used both to generate and give identity to vast quantities of interlinked media products and merchandise, resulting in a prolonged, intertextual, multimedia fictional experience' (Parody, 2011, p. 211). Modern fantasy from Tolkien onwards, we could say, became consumed by the possibilities of adaptation to other media platforms. The source texts of modern fantasy soon (although not always willingly) gave themselves up to transmedia storytelling. And over time, they became especially well-suited to franchise storytelling too, not least because modern fantasy tended to create storyworlds that were – and still are – 'vast in their scope and minute in their detail' (p. 214). This has also meant that modern fantasy, perhaps more than any other popular literary genre, has the capacity for long, elaborate storyworld afterlives.

Something happened to fantasy in the mid-1950s that enabled it to become one of the most adapted of all the popular genres. Of course, all kinds of literary works are adapted to other media platforms. This is not just something that happens to bestsellers. But the adaptation of most *literary* fiction is generally limited to conventional media such as radio, stage and screen, and it rarely leads to anything resembling franchise storytelling. An adaptation of a literary work – a novel by James Baldwin or Ian McEwan, for example – usually happens only once, maybe twice (e.g., from novel to stage to film) if things go well. And the afterlives of literary adaptations are generally short-lived and/or intermittent. It is true that a number of historical literary writers, like Jane Austen or Charles Dickens or (most obviously) Shakespeare, have managed to sustain a remarkable afterlife of transmedia adaptations over many years, crossing over into popular culture to the extent of becoming generally recognisable global brands. Shakespeare has been merchandised for a long time now, too; shops sell various Shakespearean gifts, there are festivals, events and media spin-offs, and his birthplace in Stratford-upon-Avon is, of course, a major tourist site. Shakespeare has indeed become a brand identity – Douglas Lanier calls this Shakespeare^{TM} – which means the bard is now a 'familiar figure in contemporary mass media' (Bristol, 2005, p. 72). For Lanier, Shakespeare is 'the Coca-Cola of canonical culture', 'popular culture's favourite sign of high culture' (Lanier, 2007, pp. 93, 95). So some literary authors can certainly become global brands over time. But this is unusual: it requires that author to become, literally, exceptional.

Popular genres are more likely to be adapted more frequently and extensively because they already inhabit a heavily commercialised cultural field. A bestseller already implies a large readership and, especially these days, global circulation; this can happen quickly and other forms of entertainment media can immediately (or soon afterwards) capitalise on that work's success. But to write in a popular genre by no means guarantees these things. Many romance or horror or science-fiction novelists sell modestly and are never adapted to other media platforms. When they are, they too become exceptional: think of Ian Fleming's James Bond novels or Agatha Christie's detective fiction, both of which are regularly and routinely adapted to film, video and board games, comic strips, theatre and television. Fleming and Christie also give us another reason why some popular genre writers more readily lend themselves to transmedia storytelling. These writers produced a series of novels devoted to the same one or two central characters, releasing them at regular intervals over an extended period of time: in Fleming's case, roughly one novel a year for fourteen years (from 1953 to 1966). A sustained investment in a character (Bond, Poirot, Miss Marple, etc.) makes it easier to transition from popular genre to adaptation, brand and franchise. Adaptations, as Simone Murray reminds us, require both creative and *financial* investments; they place literary works in a transactional 'cultural economy' where the author becomes one of many players in an 'interdependent network of agents' that also involves corporate money, advertising revenue and licensing agreements (Murray, 2012, p. 5). The steady release of new novels in a character-based series helps make the narrative sequence identifiable and familiar over the longer term. It builds up an ongoing, coherent storyworld, and this enables writers and the entertainment media corporations that financially invest in them to anticipate the possibility of failure or success and to plan accordingly.

Modern fantasy also learnt to do this, following the example of J. R. R. Tolkien, who published *The Lord of the Rings* in three volumes, released one after the other at (ir)regular intervals in 1954 and 1955. The novels themselves were a delayed sequel to *The Hobbit*, published almost twenty years earlier in 1937. In the meantime, Tolkien had been drafting an elaborate series of prequels, many of which were collected and published posthumously by his son Christopher as *The Silmarillion* (1977). Christopher Tolkien went on to curate and publish a further twelve volumes of *The History of Middle-Earth*, as well as numerous other editions of his father's stories, translations and essays, ending in 2018 with *The Fall of Gondolin*, one of the original 'lost tales'. The Tolkien Estate is the family's legal company (Christopher Tolkien resigned as its director in 2017), and it has made a sustained creative and financial investment in Tolkien's work over a considerable period of time, dealing with, among other things, the pressure to license and adapt that work into other media platforms – something that began relatively early on when Tolkien sold the film rights to *The Hobbit* and *The Lord of the Rings* to United Artists (UA) in 1969.

This book will look at Tolkien's work and its various transmedia afterlives, where what Kristin Thompson has called 'a previously despised genre' – modern fantasy – went on to become nothing less than a 'major international franchise' (Thompson, 2007, pp. 18, 275). It will also look at J. K. Rowling and George R. R. Martin, as two more contemporary examples of modern fantasy writers who have developed extensive transmedia portfolios out of their genre – and who further complicate and significantly extend the relationship between popular fiction, adaptation, merchandising, brand and franchise. One of the arguments in this book is that the fantasy genre after Tolkien worked by investing in its characters over the longer term, releasing long (sometimes very long) and often meandering novels one after the other almost compulsively and in a potentially never-ending way. (Some modern fantasy novelists, such as Robert Jordan, have died with their series still incomplete.) Modern fantasy novelists not only produce sequels but also prequels and elaborate back histories, as Tolkien did, expanding the reach of their narratives through explanatory notes and various digressions and spin-offs, elaborating the genealogies of families and dynasties (and often species), introducing and exploring new geographies and landscapes, and so on. Modern fantasy over the last seventy years or so can thus often seems like a perpetually incomplete project, a 'never-ending story', a matter of endlessly unfinished (literary) business. Yet despite all this – or more likely because of it – the genre continues to be adapted across a remarkably wide range of media platforms. Entertainment media corporations invest massive amounts of money into modern fantasy; some of the entertainment franchises that have built up around this genre are among the most lucrative in the world.

There is another key aspect of modern fantasy that makes its adaptation to other media platforms an attractive proposition: the development of a fully realised 'secondary world'. There are two ways of getting into a secondary world in fantasy novels. The first is to go through a portal. This is how some early fantasy takes its characters into other worlds – for example, Lewis Carroll's *Alice's Adventures in Wonderland* (1865), George McDonald's Christian fantasy *Phantastes* (1858) or, later on, David Lindsay's *A Voyage to Arcturus* (1920). J. K. Rowling's *Harry Potter* novels are portal fantasies. So is C. S. Lewis's *The Lion, the Witch and the Wardrobe* (1950), the first of his seven *Chronicles of Narnia* novels.

The second way of presenting a secondary world in fantasy is to create it as a self-contained space with its own species, its own geography and history, its own laws and its own languages. This is what Tolkien did in *The Hobbit* (1937) and *The Lord of the Rings* trilogy. The 'story-maker', he wrote in his essay 'On Fairy Stories' (1947), 'makes a Secondary World which your mind can enter. Inside it, what he relates is "true": it accords with the laws of that world' (Tolkien, 2001, p. 37). Fantasy novels that invent full-scale secondary worlds are sometimes also referred to as 'immersive fantasies', because they work by either immersing a character (like Carroll's Alice) or immersing a reader into a space that is radically different from reality (the 'primary world') and yet coherent in its own terms. In her book *Rhetorics of Fantasy* (2009), Farah Mendlesohn thinks that 'portal-quest' fantasies like the *Harry Potter* novels are different from 'immersive fantasies' because their 'system of magic' is not fully realised or explained (Mendlesohn, 2009, p. 63). She also thinks that Tolkien's *The Lord of the Rings* is a portal-quest fantasy rather than a secondary world fantasy, 'because most of the book takes place in a world strange to the protagonist(s), a condition that makes it very hard for them to question what they see' (p. 67). But this undervalues the former – since one of the points of the *Harry Potter* novels is to encourage its characters to *learn* about the 'system of magic', understanding more about it as the novels unfold – and misrepresents the latter, because *The Lord of the Rings* also works by ushering its characters into strange new worlds, encouraging them to understand and navigate their way through them. Mendlesohn suggests that characters in immersive fantasies need to be *antagonists* rather than protagonists, questioning what they see. But Tolkien, she argues, 'makes it very hard' for the hobbits to 'question what they see' beyond the Shire in *The Lord of the Rings* (p. 67). This misunderstands the cultural logic of immersive fantasies and, in particular, the kinds of fantasy narratives that work by continually expanding the frame of their worlds. An immersive fantasy takes its characters out of the world they are familiar with – the hobbits, like Alice or Harry Potter, have to leave their home – and asks them to comprehend another world. This means that immersive fantasies also have a pedagogical function: characters have no choice but to learn about the strange new world to which they have been introduced. Since fantasy after Tolkien presents ever-expanding strange new worlds, there is always more to learn and more to experience.

The emphasis on immersion is one reason why fantasy – after Tolkien – so readily lent itself to transmedia storytelling. Unlike other popular genres, fantasy novels routinely tend to give their secondary worlds some level of visualisation. Maps enable readers to navigate their way along with the characters. Tolkien himself provided drawings and maps for the first edition of *The Hobbit*, adding full-colour plates later on; he also worked with his publisher to design the dust-jackets for *The Lord of the Rings* trilogy. Maps, illustrations and visual motifs help the reader experience a sense of immersion in an imagined world. They can also work as a way of facilitating the adaptation of fantasy narratives into visual media platforms like film, video games or newer kinds of interactive media. Oliver Grau has talked about 'virtual artworks' in terms of audience immersion, which, as he puts it, 'is characterised by diminishing critical distance to what is shown and increasing emotional involvement in what is happening' (Grau, 2003, p. 13). This might very well describe Alice's experiences in Wonderland or the hobbits' experiences beyond the Shire. But he underplays the pedagogical role of immersion in narratives like these: one becomes immersed through curiosity (so crucial to Alice, of course), by learning and wanting to learn increasingly more about the strange world one comes to inhabit.

Grau notes that virtual reality is immersive because it creates 'a plausible "as if" that can open up utopian or fantasy spaces' (p. 15). The expression 'as if' suggests something preposterous or impossible (think of the Californian teenager Cher's catchphrase in the 1995 film *Clueless*), but it also recalls what Samuel Taylor Coleridge in 1817 had called a 'willing suspension of disbelief', required so that people could have 'poetic faith' in the truth of strange or extraordinary literary events, 'these shadows of imagination' (Coleridge, 1834, p. 174). Tolkien used the term 'suspension of disbelief' in 'On Fairy Stories' to express what readers need to do when they enter the secondary worlds of fantasy. In his book *As If: Modern Enchantment and the Literary Prehistory of Virtual Reality* (2012), Michael Saler argues that Tolkien's work requires a kind of unspoken collaboration between writer and reader, one 'that promotes lucidity as well as wonder, [producing] a specifically modern form of enchantment that delights but does not delude' (p. 160). Saler takes his notion of 'as if' from Hans Vaihinger's influential 1911 book *The Philosophy of 'As If'*; he also draws on Vaihinger's term 'fictionalism' to make the general point that modern imaginary worlds by the time of Tolkien enabled something more than a 'willing suspension of disbelief' because those worlds might 'continue to be "inhabited" long after the tale has been told' (p. 28). This is what Saler means by the prehistory of virtual reality, and it helps us think a little more about why modern fantasy so readily lends itself to immersion – and why it might generate a storyworld afterlife.

Immersion is often taken as a naïve form of reading, an emotional reaction that strips the reader of critical distance. It is sometimes contrasted with the so-called alienation effect – the Brechtian imperative of difficult or avant-garde modernist literary texts that were designed precisely to *prevent* immersion in a narrative. Some fantasy works, like Carroll's *Alice* books, can of course confuse the usual differences between these two dispositions. (Is Alice immersed in her secondary world or is she alienated from it?) But modern fantasy generally encourages immersion as it opens up its secondary worlds and asks its characters – and readers – to learn as they go along, as Harry, Ron and Hermione do at Hogwarts or as Arya or Bran Stark do in George R. R. Martin's *A Song of Ice and Fire* novels. Immersion means learning as you go, but a popular genre like modern fantasy is also a matter of entertainment, of being 'in the game' – as the title of Martin's first novel in his series, *A Game of Thrones* (1996), tells us – of *playing*. It is both pedagogical and recreational. Video games, role-playing games (RPGs) and board games thus find particular affinities with modern fantasy, as I will note in more detail in later sections. Katie Salen and Eric Zimmerman's *Rules of Play: Game Design Fundamentals* (2004) take Carroll's *Alice in Wonderland* as a kind of prototype fantasy text for computer and video games because it introduces a character who actually gets involved in games after going through a portal (falling down a rabbit hole) but still continually struggles to learn their rules. The key is to 'adapt to the game' (Salen and Zimmerman, 2004, p. 370), to make a commitment and keep on going, no matter how difficult or challenging it becomes – just as a video-game player does when he or she moves from one level to the next or as Frodo does when he travels with Sam towards the eye of Sauron in *The Lord of the Rings*.

The same thing might be said of the fantasy novelist who labours to produce one novel after another, extending the logics and practices of a secondary world in some cases seemingly without end (and not always with the kind of rewards given to Tolkien, Rowling and Martin). For Salen and Zimmerman, players of video games – much like readers, or authors, of fantasy novels – 'know they are participating within a constructed reality, and are consciously taking on the artificial meanings of the magic circle. It is possible to say that the players of a game are "immersed" – immersed in *meaning*' (p. 452). As a consequence, both fantasy novels and video games require a sort of 'double consciousness' from readers and players. To use terms introduced in 1999 by Jay David Bolter and Richard Grusin, readers and players (and audiences generally, depending on the media platform) experience varying degrees of *immediacy* – pure immersion, to the extent that one forgets the mediation and inhabits the medium completely – and *hypermediacy*, which makes us conscious of the nature of the media platform or genre to the extent that full immersion is not possible or prohibited (rather like Carroll's Alice saying, finally, 'You're nothing but a pack of cards!').

Bolter and Grusin's book is titled *Remediation: Understanding New Media*, and it looks at the way new media platforms routinely 'honour, rival and revise' other, often older media forms: in the way a film might be an adaptation of a piece of theatre or video games might adapt a fantasy novel such as *The Lord of the Rings*. They make the general observation that '[n]o media today ... seems to do its cultural work in isolation from other media. ... What is new about new media comes from the particular ways in which they refashion older media ... to answer the challenges of new media' (Bolter and Grusin, 1999, p. 15). Although I prefer the term *adaptation* to *remediation*, I do want to suggest that this sense of media platform recycling and refashioning is indeed nowhere more apparent than with the genre of modern fantasy. In later sections I will look at the various forms and processes of media platform adaptation of the work of Tolkien, Rowling and Martin – and there are many of them. But one example is worth briefly outlining here.

The American sociologist Gary Alan Fine wrote about the rise of RPGs around thirty-five years ago, in his book *Shared Fantasy: Role Playing Games as Social Worlds* (1983). He talked about Tolkien's *The Lord of the Rings* at some length, regarding it as 'the closest literature comes to permitting an engrossment that transcends mere reading or viewing' (Fine, 1983, p. 124). By 'engrossment', Fine means something like *immersion*. Then he talked about an American academic, Muhammed A. R. Barker, a language specialist, rather like Tolkien at Oxford. Inspired by Mike Mornard's influential *Dungeons & Dragons* games (Mornard was himself much influenced by Tolkien), Barker went on to produce *Empire of the Petal Throne*, the third RPG to be published by the American game publishing company TSR, Inc., in 1975. Fine notes that Tolkien had, of course, 'never envisioned a game based on his world' (p. 124). But he draws a sustained comparison between Tolkien's novel and Barker's later RPG, based on the way both men 'describe their fantasy histories, languages, and mythologies as being *real*' (p. 131). Fine's commentary in fact anticipates Michael Saler's use of the term 'as if' by several decades. Both Tolkien and Barker, he writes, 'treat their creations *as if* they are real, maintaining their "fabric of belief", and that they themselves are only historians, writing the record of a civilisation' (p. 131). We can say that Barker's 1975 RPG, innovative during its time, was a transmedia adaptation of a series of fantasy novels published twenty years earlier – new media refashioning old media.

This, of course, is adaptation as small-scale practice. It doesn't in itself explain why Tolkien's fantasy novels – along with Rowling's *Harry Potter* novels and George R. R. Martin's *A Song of Ice and Fire* series – went on to become major, lucrative multimedia franchises. So what exactly is a media franchise? The term describes the corporate ownership of a collection of media (films, television, games, etc.) and merchandise, all derived from a source text, an original creative work. These days, these are usually works of genre fiction (especially fantasy and science fiction) or children's fiction. A franchise, as Janet Wasko and Govind Shanadi put it, is 'a property or concept that is repeatable in multiple media platforms or outlets with merchandising and tie-in potential' (Wasko and Shavadi, 2006, p. 23). It is a matter of owning the rights and selling the licences, which means that a franchise is also very much about media ownership and control over intellectual property. This, in turn, means that franchises are both expansive and restricted. For Kyle Meikle, adaptations of popular genres like modern fantasy can work to 'kick-start' franchises, which then turn them into 'official constellations, affiliated, incorporated, and copyrighted through the business of horizontal and vertical integration' (Meikle, 2019, p. 16). One of the highest revenue-producing media entertainment franchises in the world derives from A. A. Milne's *Winnie the Pooh* (1926) and *The House at Pooh Corner* (1928). Disney bought the rights to Milne's character in the mid-1960s and has since been adapting the original stories in film, television and comic books, and merchandising them through theme parks, soft toys, gifts, games and clothing, with copyright on the ownership due to run out in 2026. This may not mean, of course, that their storyworld afterlife will come to an end.

The *Harry Potter* media franchise is ranked about tenth or eleventh in the world; the Tolkien/Middle-Earth/*The Lord of the Rings* franchise is ranked around twenty-first. In his book *Adaptations in the Franchise Era* (2019), Meikle in fact uses the Warner Bros. film *Harry Potter and the Sorcerer's Stone* (2001) and the Harry Potter prequel spin-off film *Fantastic Beasts and Where to Find Them* (2016) as the means of providing a framing chronology for his discussion of 'the imbrication of adaptation and franchising' in recent corporate entertainment media history (Meikle, 2019, p. 7). Spin-offs, sequels, prequels and 'the constellations of licensed products in media franchising' are sometimes referred to as 'paratexts' (Gray, 2010, p. 6; Johnson, 2013, p. 9), to draw on a term once used by the structuralist literary critic Gerard Genette to refer to pretty much anything that addressed or engaged a source text in some external way – from a book's cover design and illustrations, to interviews with the novelist, publicity announcements, explanatory notes, critical commentary, even a book's title and the name of the author. For Genette, some paratexts appear with a source text at the exact same moment of its original publication (e.g., the author's name, the title, the cover design, perhaps a foreword, etc.), while others appear later on, accruing around a text to give it new value, new meaning and possibly even new audiences (Genette, 1997, p. 5). These latter kinds of paratexts provide the afterlife to a source text's storyworld. In a certain precise sense, a media entertainment franchise is built around paratextual activity, we might even say *hyper-paratextual* activity. The more paratexts it can produce in different places over an extended period of time – various kinds of adaptations across a range of media platforms, an increasingly diversified range of merchandise – the more successful it can be. It helps if a media entertainment franchise is already large enough to deploy methods of promotion and distribution that work both locally and globally, producing what Meikle calls 'an international currency of recognition' (Meikle, 2019, p. 11) for the source text-as-brand.

Many commentators over the last twenty years have discussed media entertainment franchises and the transmedia adaptation of original creative works. Eckart Voights-Virchow prefers the term 'citability' to 'adaptation' – from the Latin *citare*, to set (something) into motion. (Interestingly, it can also mean 'to summons' or 'to sue' – useful to remember when the copyright of a creative work is infringed, as we will sometimes see in later sections.) For Voights-Virchow, 'adaptation' means the original creative work or source text is 'brought into movement' (Voights-Virchow, 2017, p. 73). An adaptation reanimates that original work, and it also retains, at the very least, a citational relationship to it, although it can cite other previous adaptations as well (as the more recent James Bond films often do in relation to earlier Bond films, or as Peter Jackson did in his film adaptations of *The Lord of the Rings* (2001, 2002, 2003), as I will note in Section 3). For an entertainment media franchise, one adaptation is, of course, never enough. 'Franchises encourage serialisation', Voights-Virchow writes, 'as they create a great demand for "aggregate texts" ... text clusters or text "remixes" ... that operate in transmedial storyworlds and create a sustained and intensified experience of fictional worlds on the part of the consumers' (p. 67). Entertainment media franchises – just like modern fantasy novels – require long-term investments in characters, their relationships and the predicaments they find themselves in. There must be some level of continuity here but also enough latitude to 'remake' the characters according to the prevailing sociocultural dispositions of the time. Voights-Virchow looks at Lewis Carroll's Alice books, noting that Carroll himself had produced a sequel (*Through the Looking Glass* (1871)) to his original work. The first film of *Alice in Wonderland* was made in 1903; since then, 'the Alice books have transformed into a multimodal transmedia storytelling franchise that uses platforms such as computer games, comics, TV animation, 3D CGI movies and rock songs. Alice is everywhere' (Voights-Virchow, 2017, p. 70). Her character has gone 'viral' because she is now a global brand, just like Harry Potter (although, since she is out of copyright, Alice may be more pliable, more able to be creatively 'remade').

I have noted that the phrase 'transmedia storytelling' is often used to describe the adaptation of a source work or text into other media platforms. But how much transmedia storytelling can a media franchise produce? And for how long? Media entertainment franchises always run the risk of saturating the marketplace with versions of the same story, the same characters. But the point of saturation (i.e., how many versions can we tolerate?) is always difficult to determine. For Henry Jenkins, 'There has to be a breaking point beyond which franchises cannot be stretched, subplots can't be added, secondary characters can't be identified, and references can't be fully realised. We just don't know where it is yet' (Jenkins, 2006, p. 127). There is a view among some fans, for example, that the Harry Potter franchise finally crossed a line, producing too many spin-offs, too many prequels, too much para-textual commentary. For Jenkins, 'there are strong economic motives behind transmedia storytelling' (p. 104) – an obvious point to make, of course, but one that perhaps too rigidly polarises financial investment and creative input, especially in the already commercial field of popular genres like modern fantasy. Is franchise storytelling simply driven by economic concerns and considerations? What are the limits it sets for itself? Jenkins has talked about 'media convergence', by which he means 'the flow of content across multiple media industries' and 'the cooperation between multiple media industries' in popular storytelling (Jenkins, 2006, p. 2), which can significantly extend the afterlife of a source text. 'Media convergence' underplays the level of competition *between* media platforms – and media companies and corporations – when they claim the adaptation of an original creative work for themselves. But Jenkins's example of collaboration is an interesting one. He quotes Danny Bilson, the then vice president of intellectual-property development at the American video-game company Electronic Arts, who said that an original creative work 'needs to be conceived in transmedia terms from the start' – that is, as part of 'a larger storytelling system' (p. 105). This is, of course, something entertainment media companies need to say for their own justification and well-being. But Electronic Arts only held the rights to the video-game adaptations of Peter Jackson's films, not Tolkien's novels, for reasons I will elaborate on in Section 3. Already, the heady ideals of 'media convergence' are compromised. Neil Young, an executive producer at Electronic Arts, tried his best to turn the situation into something positive: 'I wanted to adapt Peter's work for our medium', he is quoted as saying, 'in the same way that he has adapted Tolkien's work for his' (p. 107). In the event, EA produced two successful video games based on Jackson's three films of Tolkien's novels: *The Lord of the Rings: The Two Towers* (2002) and *The Lord of the Rings: The Return of the King* (2003). Jenkins notes that EA imported 'thousands of "assets" from the film production into the game, ensuring an unprecedented degree of fidelity to the details of Tolkien's world (p. 105). But he means the details of *Jackson's cinematic adaptation of* Tolkien's world: where the video games in this case (to recall Voights-Virchow's term above) work essentially as citations of a citation.

The notion of 'media convergence' is true enough for the way franchises work, which often has to do with sharing (i.e., selling or licensing) brands from one franchise to another as a way of both prolonging and proliferating a creative work's afterlife. Cross-franchise deals might be relatively elaborate – for example, the LEGO Harry Potter video games (2010, 2011) developed by the British video-game company Traveller's Tales and published by Warner

Bros. and Feral Interactive (for the OS X version), which were made available across a range of game consoles, including PlayStation, Nintendo and Xbox. LEGO models had in fact appeared with the release of the first *Harry Potter* film in 2001 and may still be continuing in the wake of the spin-off *Fantastic Beasts* films. Media convergence can be productive and lucrative, capitalising on the brand of a popular literary genre (and character) and diversifying it across media entertainment platforms through what we could think of as a horizontal 'system' of adaptation. But there is a tendency now to emphasise not 'convergence' between media so much as the *differences* between media platforms as they go about their business of transmedia storytelling. Commentators often emphasise the specificity of the processes, formats and values at work when the adaptation of a story is set into motion through a particular media platform, like cinema or video games. Each media platform structures an adaptation according to its own requirements and capacities – its creative, technical and financial limits and possibilities. A video game produced in 2002 will obviously represent its storyworld differently than a novel published in 1954 or 1955. Anthony Smith makes a version of this point in his book *Storytelling Industries* (2018): 'that the unique characteristics of traditionally differentiated media are essential to an understanding of contemporary popular narratives and wider media culture in the twenty-first century' (Smith, 2018, p. 1). And yet the source text itself, the original creative work, doesn't disappear in the process. Adaptations always create *relationships* to their source texts; they both cite it and transform it. The question of their faithfulness to the source text is open in some ways and closed in others; some adaptations might even make a point of stressing their *fidelity* to a source text, as if an adaptation should at the same time be an act of reverence or homage. Clare Parody has suggested that franchise adaptations are 'open-ended' and 'diffuse', with the capacity to 'roam freely through a franchise's textual array' in a way that says more about the 'entire franchise multitext' than it does about the source text itself (Parody, 2011, pp. 211, 212). This is an important perspective to take on board, but it is also a broadly postmodernist view that risks overstating an adaptation's capacity (even when it is produced through a franchise) for freedom of movement and trajectory. For Simone Murray, on the other hand, fidelity is in any case often and necessarily a prioritised component of an adaptation, no matter what the media platform might be.

Subsequent sections in this book will look more closely at Tolkien, J. K. Rowling and George R. R. Martin, their fantasy novels and the ways in which these have been adapted, merchandised and franchised – that is, their afterlives as forms of transmedia storytelling. But the next section will turn to modern fantasy itself to consider what exactly *did* happen to the genre in the mid-1950s and afterwards to make it so long-lasting, so expandable – so *epic* – and so adaptable to other entertainment media platforms.

2 The Afterlife of Modern Fantasy

I suggested in the last section that something happened to the fantasy genre in the mid-1950s that enabled it to make the shift from a marginal popular literary genre to a creative source for some of the largest entertainment media franchises in the world. Nicholas Birns remarks that prior to Tolkien, the fantasy genre was found 'either in minor writers or on the margins of major oeuvres' (Birns, 2018, p. 1). But as Edward James has noted, 'After 1955 fantasy writers no longer had to explain away their worlds by framing them as dreams, or travellers' tales, or by providing them with any fictional link to our own world at all' (James, 2012, p. 65). Secondary world fantasy somehow became 'normalised' and accepted, rather than weird (as in 'weird fiction') or eccentric, and transitioned into other media platforms almost immediately. For Tom Shippey, Tolkien is the originating figure here, so influential and all-encompassing that Shippey calls him the 'author of the century' (Shippey, 2000). This is indeed a grand claim to make, especially about someone who wrote fantasy novels. It might be worth noting, a little cynically perhaps, that Shippey's claim in fact had some level of corporate media authorisation. His two books on Tolkien, *The Road to Middle-Earth: How J. R. R. Tolkien Created a New Mythology* (1982, revised and expanded edition 2003) and *J. R. R. Tolkien: Author of the Century* (2000), were in fact published by Rupert Murdoch's HarperCollins, which took over Tolkien's original publisher Allen & Unwin in 1990 and has not only reprinted and published all of Tolkien's works but also published some works *about* Tolkien (presumably only the approving ones). It is also worth noting that Shippey taught Old and Middle English at Oxford, just as Tolkien had done – he drew on Tolkien's syllabus there – and then in 1979, again like Tolkien, Shippey became Chair of English Language and Medieval English Literature at the University of Leeds. This is in itself an interesting version of what we might call a paratextual afterlife: the critic's career repeats (with differences, of course) the career of the author to whom he pays tribute.

Shippey's emphasis on Tolkien's towering influence sits uneasily with his claim elsewhere that Tolkien was an 'amateur' writer whose sprawling works 'cannot be imitated on screen' (Shippey, 2003, p. 71). There is a tendency here to valorise Tolkien as resistant to transmedia storytelling –

the 'amateur' literary writer at Oxford versus 'professional' global entertainment media corporations – which, as I will note in the next section, was simply not true. We can think of the kind of adulatory criticism that Shippey has produced in his books about Tolkien as paratextual on the one hand – all literary criticism is paratextual – and a way of returning to the author as an authentic source or origin prior to media platform adaptation on the other. The radio dramatist and *Guardian* reviewer Andrew Rissik is one of several commentators who have been critical of Shippey's attempt both to rescue Tolkien from 'literary snobs' who disparage the fantasy genre and to claim Tolkien for literary greatness:

> Shippey wants to feel that his own enthusiasm, which is for morally serious fantasy of the kind Tolkien pioneered, is worthy of a place up there at the top table alongside the totemic great names of the western canon. ... The trouble is, it's not just literary snobs who don't accept Tolkien as one of the greatest writers of the last century. Almost no one does, except the hard-core Tolkien addicts who've elevated his books to the status of a cult. (Rissik, 2000)

But this counterclaim is closer to Shippey's account than it imagines, since it simply replicates the old view of fantasy as a genre at odds with the world, as something not quite normal: only a 'hard-core' addict could like it.

The view of Tolkien as an 'amateur' invested only in literary writing and no other media itself runs the risk of perpetuating the once-conventional view of fantasy as a minor, eccentric genre. But Shippey makes Tolkien play out another role that allows us to think about the afterlife of the genre in a different way. For Shippey, Tolkien is so original – developing a 'new mythology' etc. – that every fantasy novelist in his wake can only be derivative, condemned simply to reproduce all the books that Tolkien himself had introduced to the genre. A brief discussion of the American fantasy writer Terry Brooks's 'generally derided, but still commercially successful, *The Sword of Shannara*' books – a proliferating, multi-novel series first published in 1977 and apparently still going – leads Shippey to conclude that Brooks is really just a 'diluted' version of Tolkien (p. 319).

Shippey likes another American fantasy novelist, Stephen R. Donaldson, a little better, regarding him as 'much more original' but still indebted to Tolkien to the point of unconscious reproduction (p. 321). This leads Shippey to talk not about adaptation and afterlives in modern fantasy but about imitation almost to the point of plagiarism: 'in some cases', he writes, 'Tolkienian words, and images, are learned so early and so thoroughly, possibly by compulsive re-reading, that they become internalised, personal property rather than literary debt. ... It is a strange but not entirely unwelcome thing to see in an age of individual authorship and defended copyright' (p. 322). This seems to say a couple of contradictory, albeit interesting, things. First, the view that we are somehow still in 'an age of individual authorship and defended copyright' is at best only partially true – since authors are not 'individuals' and authorial copyright has continually been under assault, as we will see in the case of the fantasy genre itself in later sections. Second, Shippey suggests that in any case there cannot be any 'individual authors' after Tolkien in the fantasy genre, since Tolkienian fantasy is now so pervasive that everyone reproduces its characteristics, whether they are aware of it or not. In this account, Tolkien is modern fantasy's unconscious, its (primal) father; every fantasy writer after Tolkien is, in spite of themselves, a Tolkienian.

It is worth looking at other modern and contemporary writers in the fantasy genre to get a sense not just of their relations to Tolkien but also their relations to the business of adaptation, transmedia storytelling and franchise. This will help us to see both the limits and very real possibilities of adaptation for fantasy writers – and may also shed some light on the question of Tolkien's 'originality', influence and afterlife. The best-known of Tolkien's fantasy-writing colleagues at Oxford was, of course, C. S. Lewis – although by 1954 he had taken up a chair in medieval and renaissance literature at Cambridge. Lewis's own influences in the fantasy genre included the Scottish writer George MacDonald: 'I never concealed the fact that I regarded him as my master; indeed I fancy I have never written a book in which I did not quote from him' (Latta, 2016, p. 44). This is a different, earlier kind of originating unconscious for fantasy – one that precedes Tolkien by almost one hundred years. MacDonald's *Phantastes* was published in

1858; a 1905 edition (the year of MacDonald's death) was illustrated by the Pre-Raphaelite painter Arthur Hughes. This later edition was a collaboration between writer and artist that in a certain sense was itself an adaptation of the original work; it also shows that fantasy, long before Tolkien's self-illustrated novels, could be a visual medium.

Lewis himself was disdainful of popular fiction generally, distinguishing the fantasy genre as a higher art form – available to Pre-Raphaelite painters, for example – with a long history that went back at least as far as Edmund Spenser. The 'unliterary reader', he wrote, disparagingly, 'demand[s] swift-moving narrative. Something must always be "happening"' (Lewis, 1961, p. 30). Unliterary readers were also realists, seeing 'no point in reading about "things that could never really happen"' (p. 55). Lewis underscored the higher aspirations of fantasy as a genre by calling it 'literary fantasy': as if it stood apart from the field of popular or genre fiction and well away from the realist prejudices of the 'unliterary'. Fantasy is also never fashionable, which for Lewis meant that it could be suitable for children – because 'children are indifferent to literary fashions' – even though (and here Lewis invokes Tolkien) it is at the same time, ideally, addressed to 'everyone' (p. 70). For Lewis, however, fantasy could not be adapted to other media platforms; his comment, 'Every art is itself and not some other art' (p. 28), in fact generalises the point that adaptation is nothing less than a profane act. It ruins the sacred autonomy of any discrete art form.

And yet Lewis's fantasies have been adapted over and over. His *The Chronicles of Narnia* series consists of seven novels published at regular intervals between 1950 and 1956 – another reason why something important happened to the fantasy genre around this time. These novels were illustrated by Pauline Baynes, who had already illustrated Tolkien's *Farmer Giles of Ham* (1949). In fact, Tolkien admired her artwork so much – he wrote to Allen & Unwin, 'They are more than illustrations, they are a collateral theme' (Carpenter, 2006, p. 133) – that he even wanted her to contribute to *The Lord of the Rings*. Baynes went on to illustrate other Tolkien works and reprints; her 1969 poster-map of Middle-Earth was later produced in collaboration with Tolkien. Artists' illustrations work both as forms of collaboration and a means of *adaptation*, since they transform the written text into visual images that accompany the text and yet have a life –

and afterlife – of their own as (we might say) relatively autonomous citations. As examples, we could think of John Tenniel's illustrations for Lewis Carroll's Alice stories, or E. H. Shepherd's illustrations for A. A. Milne's Winnie the Pooh stories (Shepherd was a friend of, and mentor to, Baynes). Like adaptations, illustrations both cite the original written text and exceed it. Baynes went on to illustrate for Lewis, although he was reportedly less flattering about her work than Tolkien was; he didn't think she could draw lions. Even so, she remained a key illustrator of his work, producing the cover designs for later paperback reprints and various special editions. In 1998 'she subtly water-coloured all the original line illustrations in all seven volumes to meet the demands of a generation no longer content with black-and-white pictures' (Sibley, 2008). Here, the illustrations of a series of fantasy novels are given a further afterlife some thirty-five years after Lewis's death. The afterlife of Baynes's illustrations of Lewis's work demonstrates the sheer impossibility of maintaining the view – especially in relation to modern fantasy – that 'art must be itself and not some other art'.

Lewis was notoriously against adaptations of his novels to cinema and television. 'Aslan is a divine figure', he wrote of his lion character (confirming his sense of the sacredness of his work), 'and anything . . . in the Disney line . . . would be to me simple blasphemy'; 'I am absolutely opposed . . . to a TV version. . . . Anthropomorphic animals, when taken out of narrative into actual visibility, always turn into buffoonery, or nightmare' (cited in Edwards, 2007, p. 265). Authorising the adaptation of characters to other media platforms to make them 'visible' was pretty much impossible for Lewis, who valorised literary writing as an end in itself. But in spite of his misgivings, the Narnia novels have had a remarkable illustration and screen afterlife. The first television adaptation was a ten-part series by ABC Television in 1967, where the animal characters were played by costumed actors. An eighteen-part BBC television adaptation ran from November 1988 to December 1990, with some animals again portrayed by actors in costume but also with animated creatures, including the lion, Aslan; the teleplay was written by the respected Australian playwright Alan Seymour. Various stage adaptations include the poet Adrian Mitchell's centennial adaptation of *The Lion, the Witch and the Wardrobe* for the Royal Shakespeare Company in 1998 and

Robert Goold's 'rougher, more elemental telling' of the Narnia story for the RSC in 2012 (Trueman, 2012). This latter adaptation also aimed to produce the novel as a spectacular event on stage, with circus-like acts and massive animal puppets. The puppet designer, Max Humphries, had 'visited the Natural History Museum, he had read books on anatomy (and) got his father to help out with the drawing' while he worked on 'form and motion' (Williams, 2012). Humphries's father, Tudor, had in fact previously illustrated a 'retelling' of *The Lion, the Witch and the Wardrobe* by Hiawyn Oram, designed specifically for younger children. It is indeed difficult to keep track of the visual afterlife of Lewis's Narnia chronicles – and the anthropomorphic afterlives of his characters (the 'Narnia bestiaries') – but we can certainly note the capacity for adaptations to stretch or reconfigure the audiences and readerships of the original creative works.

The Lion, the Witch and the Wardrobe was adapted to live action film in 2005, co-financed and co-produced by Walden Media and Disney – as if Lewis's worst transmedia storytelling nightmare finally came true. A darker sequel, *The Chronicles of Narnia: Prince Caspian*, was released in May 2008; it was less successful than the first film and cost more to produce, with $100 million spent on special effects and reportedly around $175 million on marketing and promotion around the world. This could have been the point where transmedia storytelling became franchise storytelling. But Disney then pulled out of the remainder of the series. Patrick Goldstein and James Rainey, among others, have looked at what became a 'nasty feud' between Disney and Walden Media's Phil Anschutz, 'the real estate baron and supporter of Christian conservative causes who seems to own half of America' (Goldstein and Rainey, 2009). A third film in the series, *The Voyage of the Dawn Treader*, was distributed by 20th Century Fox in 2010 (and all three films were further adapted, and promotionally linked, to video games). But Walden Media's contract with what became known as the C. S. Lewis Company expired the following year. There has been much criticism of the ties between Lewis's Christian fantasy novels and the conservative Christian values of Anschutz and his organisation: among other things, Walden Media offered 'a 17-week Narnia Bible study for children' – and Disney also got involved, appointing 'Outreach, an evangelical publisher, to promote the Christian message behind the movie in

British churches' (Toynbee, 2005). But all this does at least show us how transmedia storytelling can reorient fantasy novels, in this case transforming them into family-and-church-friendly, globally distributed, screen-based entertainment.

The transition of property rights from single author to family estate to incorporated company is something we would probably see more frequently with popular genres like fantasy (think also of the Tolkien Estate) than with literary fiction. Interestingly enough, the C. S. Lewis Company (incorporated on 19 May 1999) seems enthusiastically devoted to the task of adapting Lewis's work. In October 2018 Lewis's stepson Douglas Gresham announced a multi-year deal on the company's behalf with Netflix and Entertainment One (eOne) to produce the Narnia series in its entirety. 'Netflix seems to be the very best medium with which to achieve this aim, and I am looking forward to working with them towards this goal', Gresham has said (Ravindran, 2018): showing, at the very least, that the C. S. Lewis Company is a lot more willing to embrace transmedia storytelling than C. S. Lewis was. Mark Gordon, the president of eOne and its chief content officer for film and television, looked forward to collaborating with Gresham and others on the adaptation of Lewis's novels. 'Narnia is one of those rare properties that spans multiple generations and geographies', he has said; 'eOne and I are excited to be collaborating with The C. S. Lewis Company and Netflix, who have the capacity to translate the Narnia universe into both stellar feature-length and episodic programming. We cannot wait to get started on the multiple productions we hope to undertake' (Netflix Media Centre, 2018). This is corporate and family business collaboration at its most excitable, open to transmedia storytelling in almost any form as Lewis's fantasy 'universe' is sold around the world. There is 'media convergence' here from one point of view; from another, it is a bluntly conceived act of corporate competition. It was generally noted in media reports that Netflix's bid for the Narnia series would 'see the streaming giant go head to head' with Amazon, which in late 2017 won the rights to produce at least five seasons of *The Lord of the Rings* for television (Carr, 2019).

What can we say about the fantasy novelists that Tom Shippey had regarded merely as 'diluted' versions of Tolkien, derivative and unoriginal? The question of originality in popular genres – and in literary fiction too – is almost impossible to determine. But this book is about the adaptation of a popular genre to other media platforms, which always in any case tends to put originality into question or dispute. A writer's long-term commitment to the genre, their devotion to a narrative's elaborate longevity, is much more valuable – to themselves, to their collaborators, and to the media entertainment companies that invest in them and adapt them – than 'originality'. It is probably true that Terry Brooks's *The Sword of Shannara* novels are derivative sword-and-sorcery works. But his commitment to the novel series, which has been ongoing for over forty years, is remarkable. He has regularly and systematically produced sequels, prequels, trilogies and tetralogies. In fact, a ten-episode television series based on Brooks's second novel in the original trilogy, *The Elfstones of Shannara* (1982), premiered on MTV in January 2016. A second season followed on SpikeTV, less dependent on the novels – an 'off-book adaptation' – but it was much less popular, resulting in the cancellation of the embryonic franchise. By this time, there were a number of significant fantasy adaptations out there to compete with: *Game of Thrones*, for example, had been airing on HBO since 2011.

Other fantasy writers struggled with the possibilities of transmedia storytelling, even with high sales of their novels. Stephen R. Donaldson's *Lord Foul's Bane* (1977), the first novel in his *The Chronicles of Thomas Covenant* trilogy, was published the same year as Brook's first *Sword of Shannara* novel. By 1983, when the last novel in this first trilogy was published, Donaldson claimed he 'out sold every writer in the world' (Donaldson, 1986, p. 1). Shippey had regarded Donaldson as a derivative writer in the wake of Tolkien, but in his interesting account of the genre, *Epic Fantasy in the Modern World* (1986), Donaldson both credits Tolkien for giving modern fantasy its 'epic' qualities and criticises him for 'divorcing his work from the real world' (p. 11). For Donaldson, modern fantasy should be about what it means to be 'human'. Modern quest fantasy puts this into an existential framework as a way of confronting 'the void' and as a 'movement away from futility' (p. 8); it gives its characters tasks to complete, things to learn and a reason to keep going. Like Brooks, Donaldson has continued to produce novels in his fantasy series, the last one published in 2013. But he has mixed feelings about the adaptation of his work, for example, to film:

> Prose allows me to go inside my characters; film inherently
> looks at the characters from the outside. In other words, film
> is a fundamentally different form of storytelling, with
> entirely different strengths and weaknesses; strengths and
> weaknesses which, I suspect, are not well suited to my
> stories. . . . But I don't even have the power to say NO to
> a movie deal. Of any kind. My publisher holds the film
> rights: I don't. (Donaldson, 2005, 2008)

Here, Donaldson is an author who has given away the authority to adapt his work and who does not expect it to happen in any case. It is no doubt reassuring, then, for this author to distinguish novels *from* films rather than to see them in potentially collaborative and mutually transformative terms.

Shippey's account of the unconscious transmission of influence from Tolkien to later fantasy writers only considers male novelists. But what about women who write modern fantasy series? This book will look at J. K. Rowling in Section 4, the most successful – and most lucratively adapted – fantasy novelist in the world. Of course, just like Stephen R. Donaldson, many fantasy writers are never adapted at all, no matter how long-lasting their series might be. But as I have already noted, a significant number have been. Ursula Le Guin's influential Earthsea cycle consists of five fantasy novels published between 1968 and 2001, along with a number of short stories. All this material was gathered together and published in 2018 not long after her death in *The Books of Earthsea: The Complete Illustrated Edition*, celebrating fifty years of Earthsea narratives since Le Guin's first novel in the series. Like Tolkien and Lewis and so many other fantasy novelists, Le Guin has worked with illustrators. For example, encouraged by the publisher Joe Monti of Saga Press, she collaborated for four years with the well-known fantasy artist Charles Vess. 'I really wanted to let her see the world that was in her mind', Vess has said. 'I tried really hard to do that. That was part of our collaboration. The writer and the artist sort of become a third entity. You become something better than you are as yourself. Aesthetically better' (Moher 2018). This is adaptation (from writing to artwork) as mutual transformation. A significant number of other illustrators have visualised Le Guin's work along the way, going back to Ruth Robbins, who provided the drawings and colour cover for the first US edition of *The Wizard of Earthsea*. The publisher of this edition was Robbins's husband Herman Schien, of Parnassus Press; Schien had in fact solicited Le Guin's novel. So this is a publisher-author-illustrator collaboration along similar lines to Le Guin and Vess. Robbins's cover art was of particular significance, because it gave the novel's protagonist, Ged, a brown face. 'A great many white readers in 1967 were not ready to accept a brown-skinned hero', Le Guin wrote in 2012; 'I didn't make an issue of it, and you have to be well into the book before you realize that Ged, like most of the characters, isn't white' (Bellot, 2018). Gabreille Bellot writes: 'To Le Guin's joyous relief, the book's original cover features an illustration by Ruth Robbins, in which Ged, faintly resembling a figure from either a medieval painting or Art Deco, has a soft "copper-brown" complexion. It was "the book's one true cover," she said fondly' (Bellot, 2018).

The turn to racial diversity in modern fantasy is a reaction *against* the influence of earlier writers like Tolkien and Lewis, whose characters, although they may very well be diverse in terms of species and language, are invariably white. Indeed, in *The Lord of the Rings* the wizard Gandalf becomes increasingly *whiter*: the colour signifies a dramatic increase in his power and influence. In December 2004 the Sci Fi Channel screened a two-part adaptation of the Earthsea novels by Gavin Scott. (Two years earlier, Scott had adapted Marion Bradley Zimmer's Arthurian fantasy *The Mists of Avalon* (1983) for TNT.) But Le Guin responded critically in print, casting herself as an author who felt left out of the collaborative process of novel-to-screen adaptation and who then watched her novels become 'whitewashed' and attached to a Tolkienian / northern European tradition that Le Guin, as an American fantasy writer, did not share. She wrote:

> The fantasy tradition I was writing in came from Northern Europe, which is why it was about white people. I'm white, but not European. My people could be any color I liked, and I like red and brown and black. . . . As an anthropologist's daughter, I am intensely conscious of the risk of cultural or ethnic imperialism – a white writer speaking for nonwhite

people, co-opting their voice, an act of extreme arrogance. In a totally invented fantasy world, or in a far-future science fiction setting, in the rainbow world we can imagine, this risk is mitigated. That's the beauty of science fiction and fantasy – freedom of invention. But with all freedom comes responsibility.

Which is something these filmmakers seem not to understand. (Le Guin, 2004)

In recent years some adaptations of fantasy novels have chosen to make racial diversity more visible rather than less, and more structurally appropriate to whatever conflicts and struggles their narratives present. Through her feisty werewolf characters, Stephenie Meyer's four *Twilight* novels (2005–8) drew attention to the Native American Quileute Nation from the northwestern coastal edge of Washington State, USA. The massive success of these vampire fantasy novels and the films that immediately succeeded them (2008–12) – five in total, with the last novel *Breaking Dawn* split into two parts – meant increased public awareness of the Quileute Nation, including tours, merchandising and so on. But it has also brought criticism of their representation of Native Americans as tied to wild animals and an untamed nature (in contrast to the urbane sophistication of the vampires of the Cullen family) and for the general lack of consultation 'on projects where the Quileute name and culture are used to market products' (Riley, 2010). This is again an issue of collaboration, or lack of it, when novels are produced and adapted to other media platforms – and when property rights can be robustly defended in some instances and trampled over in others. Racial diversity remains an issue in the *Twilight* novels, where the vampires themselves are white, 'pale', 'translucent', 'sparkling' and the central romance is between two white protagonists, with Bella inevitably rejecting the Native American Jacob. Catherine Hardwicke was hired by Summit Entertainment to direct the first *Twilight* film, reportedly working closely with Meyer and scriptwriter Melissa Rosenberg. But she later complained that Meyer had resisted her call to diversify the film's cast: 'Meyer pointed to the books to prove to Hardwicke why her cast could not be diverse, referencing a line about the vampires that described them as having "pale glistening skin"' (Sharf, 2018). Meyer eventually approved the casting of Kenyan-American actor Edi Gathegi in the role of Laurent; clearly, the racial diversity of modern fantasy novels is (at least to a degree) contestable, and changeable, through transmedia adaptations.

We will see more examples of this in the casting for the theatre sequel to Rowling's *Harry Potter* novels, *Harry Potter and the Cursed Child*; the principal characters in the *Harry Potter* films, on the other hand, much like in HBO's *Game of Thrones* series (think of Daenerys Targaryen), remain pretty much white all over. Another female American fantasy novelist is worth mentioning here, since her involvement with transmedia storytelling is comparable to Meyer's. The Mississippi-born Charlaine Harris set her own vampire fantasy novels – known collectively as *The Southern Vampire Mysteries* – in a fictional small provincial town in northern Louisiana called Bon Temps. There are thirteen novels in the series, with one novel published around the same time every year from 2001 to 2013 – so the series has had a long life. The central character, Sookie Stackhouse, is a white girl with a southern family history of slavery; the vampire she falls in love with is also white and fought as a Confederate soldier during the Civil War. The novels mix a dizzying array of species, but the human characters are racially homogeneous. 'Blacks didn't come into Merlotte's much', Sookie says about the bar where she waitresses (Harris, 2001, p. 151). The series' only African American character, Lafayette, is murdered at the beginning of the second novel, *Living Dead in Dallas* (2002). But when Alan Ball adapted Harris's novels as a television series for HBO titled *True Blood*, two important cast changes were made. Lafayette became a major character with his own, prolonged narrative strand, and a minor figure in the novels, a white girl named Tara Thornton, was played by the African American actor Rutina Wesley and transformed into a volatile, disaffected figure who constantly challenged racism in the Deep South until her death in the final season. When she introduces herself in the first episode of season one, she notes that she is 'named after a plantation'. Interestingly, Tara is the name given to the antebellum mansion in Margaret Mitchell's epic Civil War novel *Gone with the Wind* (1936).

Various subgenres of modern fantasy – especially those involving inter-species romance – have been the province of a significant number of women writers over the last twenty years, some of whom, like Meyers and Harris, have been successfully adapted to screen. An interesting recent success in fantasy/romance/horror has been Deborah Harkness's bestselling *All Souls Trilogy*: *A Discovery of Witches* (2011), *Shadow of Night* (2012) and *The Book of Life* (2014). Harkness is a historian of science and medicine at a University of Southern California campus, specialising in the cultural and intellectual history of early modern Britain. Her first academic book, published by Cambridge University Press in 1999, was about the famous Elizabethan alchemist and occult philosopher John Dee, often taken as a model for Shakespeare's magician Prospero in *The Tempest* and, much later, Tolkien's wizard Gandalf and Rowling's Professor Albus Dumbledore. Among other things, Dee attempted to converse with angels. His angel diaries are held in the British Library and Oxford University's Bodleian Library; Harkness seems to have drawn attention to them possibly for the first time. The heroine of *A Discovery of Witches* is Diana Bishop, a professor of history at Yale University who, while doing some research in the Bodleian Library, discovers a mysterious, enchanted manuscript. Diana turns out to be a witch; her discovery attracts the attention of other witches, as well as daemons and vampires – one of whom is Matthew Clairmont, a biochemist and fellow of Oxford's All Souls College. The romance between Bishop and Clairmont compares with the romance between, say, Bella and Edward in Meyers's *Twilight* novels; their persecution by the Congregation (a council of witches, vampires and daemons) might also recall the role of the Volturi in Meyers's series. But the *All Souls Trilogy* has some distinctive features, not least of which is its links to Elizabethan England: unlike Tolkien's *The Lord of the Rings*, this is not a medievalist fantasy. Harkness has already produced paratextual spin-off books related to her series, including *The World of All Souls: The Complete Guide to a Discovery of Witches, Shadow of Night, and The Book of Life* (2018), which gives synopses and descriptions of characters, creatures, organisations and locations; accounts of science and magic; and even recipes and commentaries on 'lifestyle'. This is another collaborative work, with three other contributors (all women, presumably research assistants) as well as an illustrator, Colleen Madden; it works to give the source texts their own elaborate afterlife.

The British entertainment channel Sky 1 bought the rights for the books and – seven years after the publication of the first novel in the trilogy – an eight-episode television series of *A Discovery of Witches* premiered in September 2018, with Australian actor Teresa Palmer cast as Diana. The romantic leads are white; although there are a couple of casting exceptions (e.g., Diana's aunt's partner), this is another exclusively white fantasy romance. It was adapted to screen by Oxford-educated scriptwriter Kate Brooke; executive producers for the series included Brooke, Harkness and former BBC executives Jane Tranter and Julie Gardner, now from Bad Wolf, a production company based in Cardiff and Los Angeles that produces high-end television for a global market. Bad Wolf takes its name from the *Doctor Who* TV series, which Tranter and Gardner (with Russell T. Davies) had helped to relaunch in 2005. The focus on Cardiff as a UK centre of transmedia fantasy storytelling is already apparent here, and the Bad Wolf website (www. bad-wolf.com) goes on to emphasise its partnership with the Welsh government, its role in the Welsh creative industries and its ongoing support for Welsh employment in the sector. Television production is indeed a collaborative process, and in the case of *A Discovery of Witches*, women – including Harkness herself – make senior contributions. This production company continued its commitment to fantasy adaptations when, in July 2018, Bad Wolf and New Line Cinema announced the cast and crew for a television series adaptation of Philip Pullman's *His Dark Materials* trilogy, *Northern Lights* (1995) – titled *The Golden Compass* in the United States – *The Subtle Knife* (1997) and *The Amber Spyglass* (2000).

Both Harkness and Pullman have produced fantasies based in Oxford, where Tolkien had worked – a hidden, occulted Oxford that in Pullman's case in particular is already adapted to cultural logics of the genre. His character Lyra's Jordan College is actually Exeter College, for example, where Tolkien had studied English language and literature as an undergraduate. (Readers of *His Dark Materials* can book 'Philip Pullman's Oxford Official Tour'.) The first novel in a spin-off trilogy, *La Belle Sauvage*, was in fact launched at the Bodleian Library (renamed as the

'Bodley' in the novel) in October 2017. Another book, *Lyra's Oxford* (2003), offers a short sequel to *The Amber Spyglass* as well as maps and other material, with wood-cut engravings by John Lawrence. Pullman seems entirely open to the adaptation of his work, the complete opposite to C. S. Lewis: 'It's been a constant source of pleasure to me to see this story adapted to different forms and presented in different media', he has said; 'It's been a radio play, a stage play, a film, an audiobook, a graphic novel – and now comes this version for television' (Bad Wolf 2018). In fact, Pullman had distanced himself from Lewis in other ways, too. In 1998, responding to the centennial celebrations of Lewis's work (and the many adaptations that accompanied this), he published an article titled 'The Dark Side of Narnia', where he admonished Lewis for his misogyny and racism (Pullman, 1998, p. 6). It is worth noting that Tolkien had also distanced himself from Lewis's fantasy novels: 'It is sad that "Narnia" and all that part of C.S.L.'s work should remain outside the range of my sympathy', he wrote in 1964, 'as much of my work was outside his' (Carpenter, 2006, p. 352). Pullman, of course, has also been critical of Tolkien: '*The Lord of the Rings* is fundamentally an infantile work', he has said; 'Tolkien is not interested in the way grownup, adult human beings interact with each other. He's interested in maps and plans and languages and codes' (Miller, 2005). This is about a contemporary fantasy novelist distinguishing himself from the kind of modern influences in the fantasy genre that Shippey had thought were all-pervasive. But in the case of Lewis, it is also to do with Pullman's criticism of the subgenre of Christian fantasy. Harkness's novels had the Congregation; Pullman's *His Dark Materials* trilogy, less subtly, has the Magisterium and the Holy Church – an oppressive, punishing institution. The emphasis for Pullman is also on young characters who develop and grow *older*, turning these novels into works of adult fantasy or perhaps young adult fantasy – something we also see with J. K. Rowling's *Harry Potter* series as it moves from the first novel to the last.

As Pullman notes, the *His Dark Materials* trilogy has indeed been adapted across multiple media platforms. In 2003–4, the London Royal National Theatre turned the novels into two three-hour stage plays; it led one reviewer to question the novels' 'adaptability' altogether, with the plays seeming 'like a clipped hedge compared to Pullman's forest' (Billington, 2004). Frances

Babbage has remarked that it is commonplace for commentators to regard theatrical adaptations of novels as 'reductive, superficial or a travesty': this is partly because the 'performative action' of theatre is ignored while fidelity to the source text is over-prioritised (Babbage, 2018, pp. 2, 15). Cinematic adaptations can draw similar kinds of criticisms. New Line Cinema's film adaptation of the first novel in the trilogy, *The Golden Compass* (2007), was in fact generally condemned along these lines: 'So much of *The Golden Compass's* effort goes into … frantic world-building', a critic in the *Guardian* noted, 'overloading us with information that we'll never actually need because they did such a bad job making the film, that the actual plot – a little girl trying to stop children from having their souls physically ripped from them – is all but buried' (Heritage, 2013). New Line Cinema had produced Peter Jackson's adaptations of Tolkien's *The Lord of the Rings* trilogy (2001–3); they may very well have expected something similar from the three novels in Pullman's *His Dark Materials*. 'They're looking for a franchise here', director Chris Weitz is reported as saying, 'meaning that if "The Golden Compass" does well, the studio will go ahead with films based on the two remaining volumes of the trilogy' (McGrath, 2007). But *The Golden Compass* was not a financial success; New Line Cinema spent around $180 million on its development but it only made around $70 in the US market. The film is generally blamed for Time Warner's decision to shut New Line Cinema down as a separately operated studio; its founder, Robert Shaye (who, a few years earlier, had given Jackson the green light to turn Tolkien's trilogy into three separate films), stepped down from the company. So this is another example of transmedia storytelling in the fantasy genre that didn't quite become franchise storytelling.

This section has looked at the way some modern fantasy novelists have been adapted to other media platforms and how these adaptations have played out, successfully or otherwise. It has also attempted to situate these novelists in the framework of Shippey's argument that Tolkien's influence on what has followed in modern fantasy has been all-pervasive. As I have noted, the origins of modern fantasy can be hard to determine. Tolkien himself was influenced by a range of *earlier* writings, some of which I will note in the next section. But I want to mention one influence here, because it is relevant to what I have been saying about both adaptation and collaboration. It is generally agreed that the work of the writer, designer and

decorative artist William Morris was particularly important to Tolkien.
They were both educated at Oxford's Exeter College, and they both studied
Old English and Old Norse, writing and translating Old Norse legends.
More specifically, as Mark Atherton suggests, 'the ideals of (Morris's) Arts
and Crafts movement surely influenced Tolkien . . . in his description of the
artistry and craftsmanship of the inhabitants of Rivendell or Lothlorien in
(*The Lord of the Rings*) or Nargothrond and Gondolin in *The Silmarillion*'
(Atherton, 2012, p. 108). The fantasy writer Lin Carter has noted that
Morris actually invented the 'imaginary world' or secondary world novel
with his 1896 fantasy romance *The Well at the World's End* (Saler, 2012,
p. 28), a quest novel that chronicles a young man's adventures as he travels
into strange new places. The novel introduces 'Gandolf, Lord of Utterbol'
and a horse named Silverfax: Tolkien's wizard Gandalf and his horse
Shadowfax are clearly citations of Morris's work. (C. S. Lewis was also
a great admirer of *The Well at the World's End*.)

Morris can also help us think about relations between adaptation,
collaboration and modern commercial production. In 1861 he set up
a company called Morris, Marshall, Faulkner & Co., producing wallpaper
designs, decorations for stained glass in churches, fabrics, furniture and so
on. He worked closely here with Charles Faulkner, Ford Madox Brown and
the Pre-Raphaelite artist Edward Burne-Jones, among others, often turning
to medieval and Arthurian narratives for inspiration. In 1875 Morris became
sole owner of the company, which went on to produce textiles and tapes-
tries; in 1877 he opened a showroom and shop at 264 (later 449) Oxford
Street, London; soon afterwards he purchased Merton Abbey Mills, a textile
factory, broadening his control over products that his firm sold 'to
a burgeoning middle-class market' (Harvey and Press, 1991, p. 122). We
can think of the work of Morris and an artist like Burne-Jones as adaptations
of medieval narratives and images, handcrafted but with an increased capacity
for mass production. The William Morris 'look' soon became a highly
marketable brand. But since it drew so heavily on older material, his work
couldn't claim to be 'original'; production was really always a form of
reproduction. 'It takes a man of considerable originality', Morris said in
1882, 'to deal with the old examples and to get what is good out of them,
without making a design which lays itself open distinctly to the charge of

plagiarism' (Thompson, 2011, pp. 103–4). This is a particularly modern response to the question of authorship, production, reproduction – and adaptation. It takes us back to Bolter and Grusin's notion of remediation, too: new media refashioning old media. And it takes us away from Shippey's view that subsequent writers in a particular genre are condemned simply to plagiarise or copy writers in the same genre who went before them.

The American academic Gary Taylor has thought about these things in relation to questions of originality and reproduction in Shakespeare's theatre, which involved collaboration between 'artisans' and also 'the labour of transforming already-existing works, already-existing text-things, into recognisably new text-things' (Taylor, 2017, p. 25). Authorship here is neither 'original' nor just a matter of pure reproduction; the emphasis instead is on 'continual modification, translation, transformation' (p. 25) – that is, *adaptation*. Taylor talks about 'artisanal labour' here (since it is essentially creative work, like writing fantasy novels), and he notes the links between the words *labour* and *collaboration*: to collaborate means sharing labour to produce (or create) something one couldn't do alone, just as fantasy writers can't produce fantasy without illustrators and, later, theatre directors, film and video game makers, designers, technicians, entertainment media corporations and their executives. Taylor's slightly awkward term for all this is 'artiginality': not simply labour as work, and not simply authorship as 'individual' and 'original', as Shippey had characterised it. Instead, labour is creative, collaborative and reproductive (drawing on older material), but it is also transformative; it *refashions*, since it turns that older material into some other, newer thing. Furthermore, this kind of labour is commercially focussed, unashamedly directed towards promotion, sales and merchandising in the marketplace. If we think in this way – about Shakespeare, about William Morris and his shop and factory, about the afterlife of novels by writers like Tolkien or J. K. Rowling or about a production company like Bad Wolf – it can help us understand transmedia story-telling a little better as a process that folds the author, willingly or not, into the wider collaborative (and these days globally distributing) imperatives of what are often still called, accurately enough, the 'creative industries'.

3 Adapting J. R. R. Tolkien

Adaptations of J. R. R. Tolkien's *The Lord of the Rings* began almost as soon as the novels were published. His publisher, Allen & Unwin, had decided to release the books in three separate volumes, one after the other. The first, *The Fellowship of the Ring*, was published on 29 July 1954, with 3,500 copies printed; it sold well enough for Tolkien to let the Scottish writer Naomi Mitchison know two months later that Allen & Unwin were already planning a reprint. The second volume, *The Two Towers* (Tolkien didn't much like the title), was published in November of that same year; and the third, *The Return of the King*, was published in October 1955. A BBC Radio adaptation came first, aired on the BBC Third Programme at the end of that year (with six episodes based on *The Fellowship of the Ring*) and again in 1956 (with six more episodes based on the final two volumes). But Tolkien was critical of this early attempt at transmedia storytelling. 'I think the book quite unsuitable for "dramatisation"', he wrote in November 1955, 'and have not enjoyed the broadcasts – though they have improved' (Carpenter, 2006, p. 228). The English poet and medievalist Terence Tiller was involved in the radio adaptation and in October 1956 had asked Tolkien what to do with the accents of the characters; among other things, Tolkien advised against giving the Orcs a 'vulgar' modern English – for example, dropping the 'aitches' (p. 254). In another letter to Tiller not long afterwards (6 November), Tolkien returned to his earlier view that the novels simply could not be 'dramatised' in another medium. Interestingly, he recognised that adaptation could indeed happen, so long as the question of fidelity to the original creative work was cast aside: 'can a tale not conceived dramatically but (for lack of a more precise term) epically, be dramatised – unless the dramatiser is given or takes liberties, as an independent person? I feel you have had a very hard task' (p. 255).

The following year – 1957, when he was sixty-five years old – Tolkien began to think a little more positively about the idea of adapting his novels for the screen. 'I should welcome the idea of an animated motion picture', he wrote to his editor, Rayner Unwin, in June, 'with all the risk of vulgarisation; and that quite apart from the glint of money, though on the brink of retirement that is not an unpleasant possibility' (p. 257). Even so, for Tolkien, adaptation didn't offer the writer much of a choice: it was either the 'vulgarisation' of cinema or, as he put it, 'the sillification achieved by the B.B.C.' radio adaptation (p. 257). In early September 1957 the American literary agent Forrest J. Ackerman visited Tolkien in Oxford to talk about producing a film adaptation of *The Lord of the Rings*. Ackerman was an important figure in the history of science fiction in the United States, contributing stories, editing anthologies, running large-scale fan societies and representing a number of key writers in the genre, including Ray Bradbury and Isaac Asimov. He was also an aficionado of science-fiction cinema, which became increasingly prominent in the 1950s. With writer Morton Zimmerman and television producer Al Brodax – who at the time was a programme developer at William Morris's Hollywood-based talent agency (no relation to the English writer and designer) – Ackerman presented a film proposal to Tolkien and produced an extended synopsis. In a letter to his children on 11 September, Tolkien seemed both interested and cautious. Interestingly, he polarised his options in a way that exactly recalls the French cultural sociologist Pierre Bourdieu's notion of the 'two principles of hierarchisation' that divide the literary field: the 'autonomous principle' ('art for art's sake') and the 'heteronomous principle' ('favourable to those who dominate the field economically') (Bourdieu, 2002, p. 77). '[I]t looks as if business might be done', Tolkien remarked. 'Stanley U[nwin] & I have agreed on our policy: *Art or Cash*. Either very profitable terms indeed; or absolute author's veto on objectionable features of alterations' (p. 261). I commented briefly on the phrase *as if* in Section 1: it turns out to be important to transmedia storytelling and the fantasy genre in more ways than one.

Tolkien read over the synopsis carefully, but this only made him all the more conflicted. Zimmerman, he complained to Rayner Unwin in April 1958, 'does not read books. ... I feel very unhappy about ... his complete lack of respect for the original. ... But I need, and will soon need very much indeed, money, and I am conscious of your rights and interests' (p. 267). For Tolkien, all adaptations must deviate from the 'original' creative work, which was regrettable – because fidelity was his priority. On the other hand, adaptations paid well. But the more he read, the less he liked it. In a letter to Ackerman, possibly in June 1958, Tolkien listed all the changes he objected to in the film synopsis: the truncation of the journey of the Ring-bearers, which 'has . . . simply been murdered'; the 'misrepresentation' of Tom Bombadil; the confusion of names; the contraction of the seasonal time scheme (pp. 271–2). 'Strider does not "Whip out a sword" in the book', he wrote; 'Aragorn did not "sing the song of Gil-galad"'; 'The Black Riders do not scream, but keep a more terrifying silence' and '*The Balrog never speaks* . . . ' (pp. 273–4). At the end of a long string of complaints, he seems to have lost patience altogether: '*Part III . . . is totally unacceptable to me* . . . ' (p. 277).

Ackerman's option on the film of *The Lord of the Rings* expired in 1959; in the meantime, Tolkien's reputation grew exponentially. Donald Wollheim's Ace Books published cheap science fiction in the United States, and Wollheim wanted the rights to publish *The Lord of the Rings* in paperback. When Tolkien refused, Wollheim went ahead and published anyway, printing Ace's own edition of the trilogy with colourful cover illustrations by Jack Gaughan (Liptak, 2013). Tolkien began to correspond with his American fans, urging them to boycott the Ace paperbacks; finally, Wollheim agreed to pay him the royalties and let the Ace edition sell out. The paperback publisher Ballantine, under licence from Houghton Mifflin, then released an 'authorised' US edition of the trilogy. By 1968 *The Lord of the Rings* had sold three million copies worldwide. Andrew Liptak notes that the popularity of Tolkien's trilogy in North America 'spark(ed) a new movement of fantasy fiction', with Wollheim's act of trans-Atlantic piracy having 'a lasting impact on the genre' (Liptak, 2013). In the late 1960s Tolkien's work was embraced by university students, progressive rock bands and the counterculture, all of whom may well have valued modern fantasy because it 'imparted a sense that another world was possible – or perhaps more importantly, believable' (Rubin, 2012, p. 267). As the specialist book dealer Rick Gekoski put it, Tolkien was 'reinvented in the sixties. . . . [He] joined the Beatles, Andy Warhol and Timothy Leary as a star in the psychedelic galaxy' (Gekoski, 2004, pp. 17–18).

In fact, the Beatles had themselves proposed a film adaptation of *The Lord of the Rings*, the third in the band's three-film deal (after *A Hard Day's Night* and *Help!*) with UA. Stanley Kubrick was approached as director; McCartney would be cast as Frodo, Lennon as Gollum, Harrison as Gandalf and Ringo Starr as Sam. Sadly, this particular 'pop' screen adaptation never materialised. But UA continued to be interested in Tolkien's trilogy, and in 1969 he sold the film and merchandising rights to them for £104,000 and a modest royalty from all future cinematic adaptations. UA was then free to do pretty much what it wanted with the novels. In 1970 it commissioned the British director John Boorman to produce a screenplay of *The Lord of the Rings*, but nothing eventuated. Six years later – three years after Tolkien's death – UA retained the distribution rights but sold the production rights for both *The Lord of the Rings* and *The Hobbit* to an independent producer, Saul Zaentz, who went on to obtain from the Tolkien estate 'the trademarks for the names of all the characters, places, and objects in the novels' (Thompson, 2007, p. 19). This is where franchise storytelling began for Tolkien. Controlling the film, stage and game rights to his work (with some qualifications), Zaentz set up his own Tolkien Enterprises in 1978; in 2010 it was renamed Middle-Earth Enterprises. In the late 1970s Tolkien Enterprises was associated with three striking animated film adaptations of Tolkien's work. The first was *The Hobbit* (1977), licensed out to Rankin/Bass Productions, an American company well known at the time for its stop-motion TV animation, much of which was produced in Japan. The *New York Times* reported that it took five years to make and cost $3 million – at the time, it was 'the most expensive animated television show in history' (Culhane, 1977). The original concept art for this film was by Lester Abrams, who took his visual influences for the characters from an eclectic range of sources: the English fantasy illustrator Arthur Rackham, Disney (for the dwarves), a self-portrait of Leonardo da Vinci (for Gandalf) and the work of Swedish artist John Bauer (Plesset, 2002, pp. 52–3), renowned for his illustrations for the annual *Among Gnomes and Trolls* folklore and fairy-tale series (1907–10, 1912–15). *The Hobbit* was also a musical; its theme song, 'The Greatest Adventure', was sung by the American folk singer Glenn Yarbrough. Musical soundtracks tied to adaptations are, of course, another kind of transmedia storytelling, with their own elaborate life and afterlife. The casting of voices is also important in animated film. Orson Bean, an American game show-host and actor who had been blacklisted in the 1950s, was cast as Bilbo Baggins. 'I didn't use a voice change to do Bilbo', he has said. 'I did an attitude change, making Bilbo kind of fussy – fussy and proper – then gradually dropped the fussiness and properness as the madness of battle really affects him' (Culhane, 1977). In the event, the animated film was well received and popular. Co-producer Arthur Rankin Jr. cast the adaptation, broadcast on NBC on 27 November 1977, as something Tolkien readers from the 1960s might even transmit to a new generation, as if the afterlife of Tolkien's novels could be found right here: 'It must have been everybody that ever read Tolkien in college stayed home with their kids that night' (Chase, 1982).

Rankin/Bass produced a sequel musical animated film, *The Return of the King: A Story of the Hobbits*, marketed by Warner Bros. and screened on ABC in May 1980. They turned to Tolkien's last novel in the trilogy because Saul Zaentz had, by this time, produced another animated film – Ralph Bakshi's *The Lord of the Rings* (1978) – based, more or less, on the first novel and part of the second, coming to an end when Gandalf and the Riders of Rohan destroy the orc army ('As their gallant battle ended, so too ends the first great tale of *The Lord of the Rings*'). Bakshi was a progressive, countercultural animator, responsible for films like *Fritz the Cat* (1972) – Hollywood's first X-rated cartoon – and *Heavy Traffic* (1973). His *The Lord of the Rings* had shot live-action scenes in Spain and traced them, frame by frame, onto animation cells for realistic effects; it employed 164 artists and cost $6 million to make (although some sources suggest $8 million). By the following year it had 'earned worldwide rentals . . . of between $45 million and $50 million, while satisfying most film critics and Tolkien cultists' (Culhane, 1981). It is a much darker adaptation than the two Rankin/Bass cartoons. 'My Mordor', Bakshi commented, 'is very much like Auschwitz. It's ashes. It's cold. It smells of the decay of humanity. The dead die and stay unburied' (Harmetz, 1978). A teacher, Chris Conkling, was hired as a scriptwriter and went through a number of drafts; the fantasy novelist Peter S. Beagle did the final revisions and the prolific film composer Leonard Rosenman did the musical score. So the late 1970s saw three reasonably successful animated films developed as adaptations of Tolkien's work. Zaentz's Tolkien Enterprises went on to expand the range of adaptations by signing a deal in 1982 with Iron Crown Enterprises, a major RPG company. *Middle-Earth Role Playing* (1984) was one of a number of their Tolkienian RPGs and board games. But

Tolkien Enterprises revoked their game licence in 1999, possibly to free it up to tie into the forthcoming Peter Jackson film adaptations; the following year, Iron Crown Enterprises was declared bankrupt.

Jackson's reputation was built around New Zealand–based splatter comic-horror films like *Bad Taste* (1987) and *Braindead* (1992). Broader critical recognition came with *Heavenly Creatures* (1994), distributed by Miramax and based on a real event – teenagers Pauline Parker and Juliet Hulme's murder of Parker's mother in Christchurch, New Zealand, in 1954. Jackson pitched the idea of making a film of *The Hobbit* to Harvey Weinstein, who was then the head of Miramax. But the film rights to *The Hobbit* were still owned, at least in part, by UA/MGM. Weinstein had been working with Saul Zaentz on *The English Patient* (1996). When he realised Zaentz owned *all* the film (and merchandising) rights to *The Lord of the Rings*, Weinstein signed a contract for the licence (in 1997), and Jackson, with his partner Fran Walsh, produced a script. The idea was to produce two films, budgeted for around $140 million, but Miramax was owned by Disney, which wanted to invest in one film only. 'Disney ran the numbers', Fran Walsh has commented, 'and they said, "Fantasy films don't make money"' (Perez, 2012). Jackson then shopped his script around, ending up at Bob Shaye's New Line Cinema, which had enjoyed earlier commercial success with the *Nightmare on Elm Street* film series. It was Shaye who suggested that Jackson produce three films, not two, releasing them one after the other, just as Tolkien had done with his novels. Jackson and Walsh, along with Philippa Boyens, then reorganised and expanded the original script to suit the new project. But there were immediate questions of risk and scale. The production costs for the first film alone exceeded $90 million; for all three films, they were around $300 million. On the other hand, merchandising licences with companies like Burger King and Barnes & Noble raised significant revenue, and since the trilogy was to be filmed, developed and produced in New Zealand/Aotearoa, the New Zealand government contributed $10 million per film in tax incentives (Lyman, 2001). The films would in fact go on to turn New Zealand, for a few years at least, into a sort of simulated Middle-Earth. They transformed the symbolic identity of an entire country, overlaying Tolkienian maps and geographies onto New Zealand/Aotearoa as the filmmakers built their sets and made cinematic claims on particular locations. Tolkien's invented Elvish language mixed with Maori in some of the commentaries during this time. The small town of Matamata on the North Island, not far from Hamilton, became 'Hobbiton'; it still functions as a tourist site (literally a 'global village'), inviting visitors from around the world to explore the movie sets and 'step into the lush pastures of the Shire^{TM}' (www .hobbitontours.com/en/). New Zealand, as the 'Home of Middle-Earth', became a marketing brand, managed and promoted worldwide by local tourism boards, Air New Zealand and so on. This is an entirely unexpected outcome of franchise storytelling and the result of a range of historically accidental things: developments in CGI technology; a recently established history of cheap, landscape-centred filmmaking in New Zealand (already tied to the fantasy genre); and the financial and creative investments of a small and otherwise remote country that welcomed the chance to become more globally visible.

In her book *The Frodo Franchise: The Lord of the Rings and Modern Hollywood*, Kristin Thompson gives a cheerily positive account of Jackson's three films, suggesting that they 'inject(ed) prestige into a previously despised genre' (Thompson, 2007, p. 275). Her commentary romanticises Jackson's elaborate cinematic adaptations of Tolkien's trilogy:

> The story has a charming David-and-Goliath quality. A Hollywood studio entrusts hundreds of millions of dollars to an eccentric, largely unknown director from a distant country where film production barely exists. He undertakes to adapt a beloved classic book with a devoted cult following – a large cult, certainly, but hardly enough to ensure box-office success for such an expensive venture. The director refuses to leave the little country, instead building a world-class filmmaking infrastructure in his neighbourhood. He shoots three long features simultaneously and creates the biggest box-office franchise in history. To top it off, despite being in the despised fantasy genre, the three parts of *The Lord of the Rings* win a total of seventeen Oscars. (p. 17)

The transformation of a series of 'cult' fantasy novels into a series of very expensive Hollywood films could certainly seem disconcerting to some commentators. In an article published in the *London Review of Books* a month before the world premiere of Jackson's first film, *The Fellowship of the Ring*, Jenny Turner wrote with some trepidation that Tolkien's 'most backward-looking and fustily word-bound of popular novels is about to become ... a ... rather literary-looking advert for a multimedia franchise a bit like *Star Wars*, only bigger' (Turner, 2001). But looking at the film trailers made her think differently, and a bit more poetically, about these screen adaptations:

> The landscapes – what they are prepared to let you see of them – have that digitally enhanced hyper-real quality more sumptuous than Technicolor, more magical than cartoons: super-icy mountains, mega-scary forests, stormier than the stormiest of skies. The effect, in current parlance, is usually called 'achingly beautiful': a deep, mysterious mixture of pain and pleasure, a yearning towards the impossible, with something delirious in it and something sublime. A deep, mysterious feeling which yet can be commodified and evoked with great efficiency by the entertainment industry, like a confection of pink sugar, like a drug ... (Turner, 2001)

The DVD set of Jackson's films contains a series of appendices, both reflecting and paying tribute to Tolkien's various appendices to *The Lord of the Rings*, where, as with Tolkien, a range of further details connected to the main project are chronicled and elaborated on, sometimes at considerable length. Here, Jackson is keen to stress the scale of his film-making, using the term 'epic' over and over. He tells us he initially thought the novels were 'unfilmable' because of their size; even so, this particular adaptation mimics the cultural logic of the original creative work (prioritising fidelity) as it embraces the sheer scale of the project. In order to bring the novels coherently onto the screen, an entire army of designers, technicians and artists were assembled, workshops were built and new CGI processes were invented. Jackson had already established Weta Digital in Wellington to do the special effects for *Heavenly Creatures*; it significantly expanded and developed for *The Lord of the Rings* films. A computer animation software package, appropriately named MASSIVE (Multiple Agent Simulation System in Virtual Environment), was invented at Weta Digital by Stephen Regelous to enable the staging of large-scale battle sequences. Weta Workshop built the armour, weapons, prosthetics, miniatures and so on, and along with the work of a range of artists, including the well-known Tolkien illustrators Alan Lee and John Howe, they created the 'look' of Middle-Earth. The costume designer Ngila Dickson – who had previously worked on the New Zealand–filmed American fantasy series *Xena: Warrior Princess* (1995–2001) – oversaw the work of forty seamstresses, creating 19,000 costumes. The composer Howard Shore wrote and produced the music for the films across a period of two years, suggesting in one of the appendices that he actually felt like Frodo: 'I had this amazing journey to take.' The notion of a 'journey' of 'epic' proportions became central to the self-presentation of Jackson's overall project, with the film-making process lasting six or seven years in total. But in the last appendix to the third film, *The Return of the King*, Jackson sentimentally reconnects with his home town of Wellington, securing it for that film's world premiere in the north island city's Embassy Theatre movie house. It leads him to refer to his trilogy as 'the biggest home movie in the world', capturing both the grand scale of these particular adaptations and New Zealand's localised 'Home of Middle-Earth' brand identity. Jackson's three films would go on to gross more than $2.9 billion worldwide; *The Return of the King* became the first fantasy film to win Best Picture at the Oscars.

Not everyone was pleased with Jackson's films. Patrick Curry's *Defending Middle-Earth* (2004) is a fantasy genre traditionalist's spirited after-the-horse-has-bolted defence of Tolkien against adaptation per se: 'Tolkien's own definition of enchantment . . . remains one of the best', he writes; 'One synonym could be, "sacred". Another might be, "NOT FOR SALE"' (Curry, 2004, p. 152). For Tolkien devotees, the trilogy is 'canonical'; any adaptation to another media platform is a departure from the

canon and judged severely. But in fact Jackson's films were deeply respectful of the novels. Various alterations were made, of course – for example,
battles were placed in climactic positions in each film; Arwen was 'upgraded
to a fully-fledged character' (O'Hehir, 2002, p. 52) to increase the number of
powerful warrior women in the adaptations; Tom Bombadil was dropped
altogether; and a new 'non-canonical' character, Lurtz, one of Saruman's
Orcs, was created. 'It's the only time in the movies that we've created
a character that Tolkien didn't actually write about', Jackson has noted;
'Because we thought we needed to personalise the leader of this band of
Orcs' (Bauer, 2002, p. 12). There were also citations in the films of other,
earlier adaptations of Tolkien, such as Bakshi's 1978 animation. And things
like the artwork for the films were in any case already forms of transmedia
storytelling. Alan Lee and John Howe were the lead conceptual artists for
Jackson's films, but they had themselves produced various illustrated editions of Tolkien's work earlier on: for example, Lee had illustrated the
lavish 1992 centenary edition of *The Lord of the Rings*, and John Howe had
illustrated Brian Sibley's *The Maps of Tolkien's Middle-Earth* in 1994. These
illustrators brought their own Tolkienian aesthetic tastes and histories to
bear on the Jackson films. A tribute article in the *Guardian* in 2018 called Lee
'the man who redrew Middle-Earth': the emphasis here is on the way
illustrations work to re-visualise a secondary world all over again in new
formats and in new ways (Barnett, 2018).

We can see here that adaptation can happen as a matter of routine across
a range of media platforms and in a variety of places: as far away as New
Zealand or much closer to Tolkien's home and the original 'canon' of source
texts. In June 2018 the Bodleian Library at Oxford curated an exhibition,
Tolkien: Maker of Middle-Earth, where a range of Tolkien source material
(draft manuscripts, letters, paintings, maps, etc.) was on public display. But
even here, we see examples of adaptation – as well as the merchandising of
transmedia products. The Bodleian produced a 'collector's edition',
Tolkien's Treasures, published 'in a custom-made presentation box' and
featuring facsimile reproductions of Tolkien material. A Tolkien shop
and showroom continues to sell Tolkien mugs, bags, rings, pencil cases
and jigsaw puzzles. Tolkien is not just an author but a highly marketable
brand, owned by key investment companies, a property for hire or for

license. The name 'Tolkien', the shop website tells us, is a registered trademark of the Tolkien Estate; it goes on to say that 'Smaug™, The Hobbit™, Bilbo Baggins™ and Arkenstone™ are registered trademarks of The Saul Zaentz Company and used by permission' (www .bodleianshop.co.uk/collections/j-r-r-tolkien).

Zaentz, New Line Cinema and Peter Jackson were involved in various disputes after *The Lord of the Rings* regarding payments, profits, and the licensed use of the Tolkien trademark. There was pressure on New Line Cinema to make a film of *The Hobbit* because it only held the production rights until 2010. In the meantime, Jackson and Bob Shaye fell out, New Line Cinema was absorbed into Warner Bros., and UA – which had retained *The Hobbit*'s world distribution rights – was absorbed by MGM. The studios finally agreed to produce two films of *The Hobbit*, but when Jackson refused to direct them, they appointed the Mexican horror film-maker Guillermo del Toro, who had recently had some success with the *Hellboy* comic book film adaptations (2004, 2008). But del Toro quit the films in mid-2010, and Jackson, his partner Fran Walsh and Philippa Boyens took over, turning two films into three: *The Hobbit: An Unexpected Journey* (2012), *The Desolation of Smaug* (2013) and *The Battle of the Five Armies* (2014). The result was another trilogy released one after the other over three consecutive years.

It is generally agreed that *The Hobbit* films were produced in a hurry – not so much a 'journey' as a quick sprint. One interview with Jackson at the time is titled, '"I didn't know what the hell I was doing" when I made *The Hobbit*' (Child, 2015): he had so little preparation time that some scenes were barely storyboarded. There was general critical agreement that three films of *The Hobbit* were too many: unlike *The Lord of the Rings*, this particular cinematic adaptation should not have been (or attempted to be) an 'epic' fantasy. They were also out of the novels' chronological order, coming after *The Lord of the Rings* films rather than before them. Jackson produced a 3D option and developed a hi-tech forty-eight frames-per-second format (twice the normal rate), but these things made little difference to the films' lukewarm reception. For A. O. Scott in the *New York Times*, the first film in the series was simply 'theme-park cinema': 'the shiny hyper-reality robs Middle-Earth of some of its misty, archaic atmosphere, turning it into a gaudy high-definition tourist attraction' (Scott, 2012). This is like two adaptations rolled into one: from novel to film to theme park. The *New York Times'* reviewer of the second film in the series, Manohloa Dargis, noted the Sherlock Holmesian joke of casting Martin Freeman as Bilbo and then using Benedict Cumberbatch's voice for the dragon Smaug, and she praises (to a degree) the invention of the Elven female warrior Tauriel, 'created to femme up the nearly all-male world' of Tolkien's novel (Dargis, 2013). But she is generally unimpressed with Jackson at his worst, a 'crushingly straight, unoriginal director who seems largely interested in topping himself with bigger, louder, more frenetic action' (Dargis, 2013). The third film, *The Battle of the Five Armies*, was the most critically received, not least for stretching out what is in fact a brief scene in the novel. Here, the *New York Times* is blunt: 'Bilbo may fully learn a sense of friendship and duty, and have quite a story to tell, but somewhere along the way, Mr. Jackson loses much of the magic' (Rapold, 2014). *The Battle of the Five Armies* was the second-highest-grossing film of 2014, but it was the lowest grossing of all the Peter Jackson Middle-Earth cinematic adaptations.

It was often pointed out that the mass of CGI effects in Jackson's later *Hobbit* films meant that these cinematic adaptations were, as one critic put it, 'overshadowed by a computer game aesthetic' (Kermode, 2014). In fact, video or computer game adaptations of Tolkien's work began relatively early on; the first computer game of *The Hobbit* was produced back in 1982, developed by Beam Software and published by Melbourne House, and it was a remarkable commercial success. But the differences between Zaentz's Tolkien Enterprises (which owned the film and merchandising rights) and the Tolkien family's Tolkien Estate (which owned the book rights) meant that transmedia storytelling was always going to be complicated. Later on, Sierra Entertainment were licensed to build a game of *The Hobbit* (2003) based on the book rights, but Electronic Arts had already purchased the movie licence connected to Jackson's films. As Alexa Ray Corriea puts it in a fascinating article about Tolkien's video game adaptations, this 'would become a symptom of video games based on Tolkien's works moving forward: the problem of dual licenses', which meant 'there were two valuable commodities on the market – two commodities of the same property that couldn't cross-pollinate or resemble one another' (Corriea, 2014). Sierra Entertainment was a holding company of Vivendi Universal Games, and while SE was producing *The Hobbit*, they published *The Lord of the Rings: The Fellowship of the Ring*, a licensed game adaptation of Tolkien's 1954 novel. It could not resemble Jackson's films: the one could not be transmediated into the other. EA had the opposite problem: its games couldn't draw on the novels. Corriea quotes Ash Monif, who worked on EA's *The Lord of the Rings: The Third Age* (2004):

> When we were planning the game, we wanted to have all these Dwarves and Dwarf armies and all that kind of stuff – and we couldn't because in the movies at the time, you only see one Dwarf, Gimli. It was very limiting to us: we had to basically get permission from Warner Bros. for everything and could only work in these very narrow confines of stuff that was in the movies. . . . We had to be creative with what we had. (Corriea, 2014)

This is franchise storytelling as a matter of restriction, not expansion.

Things changed when EA gained the rights to both the books and the films in 2006; an ambitious game was planned, *The Lord of the Rings: The White Council*, but EA later put it on indefinite hold. In March 2009, Warner Bros. gained the rights to make video games based on Jackson's films from EA, and soon afterwards, they acquired the rights from Vivendi to make games based on the novels. This enabled a single corporation to produce crossover adaptations for the first time and also to invent new, 'non-canonical' characters. An early outcome was *The Lord of the Rings: War in the North*, a 'hack-and-slash' video game developed by Snowblind Studios and published in 2011 by Warner Bros., with three playable characters – a ranger, a dwarf and an elf. It was, however, both a commercial failure and poorly received: a reviewer at Eurogamer called it 'a soulless cash-in that has little to do with its license', turning a much-anticipated visit to 'one of Western civilisation's most revered fictional settings' into a 'chore' (Matulef, 2011). In 2014 Monolith Productions – another 'interactive entertainment' subsidiary of Warner Bros. – released *Middle-Earth: Shadow of Mordor*, and in 2017 they released a sequel, *Middle-Earth: Shadow of War*. In these games, which take place somewhere in the sixty-year span that separates *The Hobbit* and *The Lord of the Rings*, a 'non-canonical' ranger, Talion, bonds with Celebrimbor, a character who was instrumental in forging the rings for Sauron and who quotes passages from Tolkien's work as the games unfold. This is adaptation as a transformative project that is also collaborative across media platforms: Jackson's Weta Workshop, for example, provided assistance with special effects. The games even drew on David Salo – a linguist who had worked on Jackson's films as the Tolkien language consultant – for the Orcs' Black Speech. Like Jackson, Michael de Plater, the creative director at Monolith, has discussed the six-year-long production of these games in terms of its 'epic scale' – more of a 'roller-coaster' than a 'journey'. The game itself is long, requiring gamer commitment: 'People are going to build stories over time, and I think the game is really going to shine when people enjoy it like that', de Plater has said (Takanashi, 2017).

Video games – and there are many more of them as far as Tolkien's storyworld afterlife is concerned – are particular kinds of adaptations that in this case break the original work down into 'layers', focus on particular characters and particular conflicts, (re)design the 'look' of the secondary world, add music, voices and a soundtrack and aim to encourage long-term player commitment and (regulated) forms of interactivity. De Plater makes this observation about the *Shadow of War* video game:

> It's an adaptation, basically. If you see almost any film or TV show or other work coming from a canon book or other original property, that's often the best way to approach that. We're as faithful as we can and as true as we can to every-thing we love and feel is in the spirit of Middle-Earth, but it's certainly our version of a lot of those books. . . . It's a kind of what-if in some ways. When you read *Lord of the Rings*, the big question that gets posed more than any other is what would happen if someone with power took up the One Ring. Gandalf is tempted. Galadriel is tempted. Boromir is tempted. Celebrimbor is our answer, in some ways, to what would have happened if Galadriel had taken the Ring

and become a dark queen in place of a dark lord.
(Takanashi, 2017)

I have previously noted that the phrase *as if* is important to fantasy because
it implies both something preposterous and the willing suspension of
disbelief required to make a fantasy's secondary world seem sensible or
comprehensible. But de Plater is talking about *what if* – that is, the ways in
which an adaptation departs from the original creative work precisely to do
something 'non-canonical'. We can call this speculative transmedia storytelling. Much of the work on Tolkien himself over the past seventy years or
more has been about annotating the canon and *extending* the canon –
through the posthumously published work edited and curated by
Tolkien's son Christopher, for example, or the elaborate guides and 'com-
panions' of Tolkien scholars like Christina Scull and Wayne G. Hammond.
But this is precisely why these adaptations of Tolkien's work have so much
to work *with* – and to depart *from*. It is the combination of regulated licences
to produce and distribute, along with the opportunity to create, to 'redraw'
and to deviate from canonical narratives and characters, that makes Tolkien
such an attractive and long-lasting *brand*. In November 2017 Amazon
confirmed its acquisition of the global television rights for *The Lord of the
Rings*. At around $250 million, this was 'the biggest TV rights deal in
history for a literary property'; as Rob Cain notes in *Forbes* magazine, it was
more or less one thousand times the amount Tolkien received when he first
sold the movie and merchandising rights to UA fifty years earlier (Cain,
2017). In March 2019 Amazon confirmed that a multi-season live-action
adaptation of Tolkien's work was in pre-production, set in the so-called
Second Age – which lasts more than three thousand years, long before the
events of *The Hobbit* and *The Lord of the Rings*. It even released an
interactive map of Middle-Earth, describing the series locations
(www.amazon.com/adlp/lotronprime) in a shameless mimicry of (or
homage to) Tolkien's famous remark in 1954, 'I wisely started with
a map' (Carpenter, 2006, p. 177). So more speculative transmedia storytelling is forthcoming, possibly scheduled, as I write, for 2021: adaptations
of and large-scale corporate investments in Tolkien's proliferating modern
medievalist fantasies continue apace into the future.

4 J. K. Rowling and the Potterverse

J. K. Rowling's *Harry Potter* novels, like Tolkien's *The Hobbit* and *The Lord of the Rings*, take a young character out of his home (albeit an adopted and abusive one) and engage him in a prolonged battle against an evil force. They involve a number of quests (or tests) but no long, 'epic' journeys. Harry moves back and forth between the real world (suburban London) and the magical world; the latter is separate from the former but routinely spills over into it. Tolkien's novels are regarded as works of high fantasy, where there is only a secondary world. But there is some debate about whether the *Harry Potter* novels are high fantasy or low fantasy (where magical events infiltrate the real world – as in, for example, P. L. Travers's *Mary Poppins* novels (1934–88), another transmedia storyworld fantasy series/franchise) or a mixture of both. There are many obvious and profound differences between Tolkien's myth-building work and Rowling's *Harry Potter* novels, but two are worth mentioning here. The first – remembering Philip Pullman's earlier complaint about Tolkien – is that as the *Harry Potter* novels unfold, readers are able to see the protagonist develop and *grow*. This meant that the novels themselves transitioned through the series, from children's fantasy to young adult and then (more or less) adult fantasy. A second difference is that the *Harry Potter* novels are not set in some distant 'medievalist' past. As I have noted, there are clearly traceable genealogies that link Albus Dumbledore to Gandalf and then to Shakespeare's Prospero and the Elizabethan figure of John Dee, and perhaps even to Merlin (Dumbledore is awarded the Order of Merlin). And of course, there are 'medievalist' features in the *Harry Potter* novels like the tournaments, the use of bestiaries, the dragons, or the reference in the first novel to the French alchemist Nicolas Flamel (who created the Philosopher's Stone). But the novels themselves are contemporary and English. They introduce what Andrew Blake has described as a sort of post-Thatcher suburban London 'retrolutionary', a boy who makes himself indispensable to the survival of an archaic English boarding school and yet who seems entirely appropriate to '1997 and after' (Blake, 2002, p. 4).

The transformation of Harry Potter from a fictional character into a brand and a franchise – one of the largest entertainment franchises in the world – is now very well known but worth rehearsing again (hopefully, a little differently) here. After publisher rejections from Penguin and HarperCollins among others, the first novel in the series, *Harry Potter and the Philosopher's Stone*, was published in the United Kingdom by Bloomsbury on 27 June 1997 in an edition of five hundred copies, three hundred of which reportedly went straight to libraries. A succession of relatively modest reprints soon followed. It was Barry Cunningham at Bloomsbury who advised Rowling to publish under the initials 'J. K.', rather than 'Jo', on the grounds that the novel seemed like a fantasy written for boys. Bloomsbury had mostly published quality literary fiction until then, but its investment in Rowling's fantasy novels turned out to be central to the company's considerable future prosperity. The first novel was in fact already conceived as part of a longer series of books built around the growth and development of the protagonist. As Cunningham has commented, on his initial meeting with Rowling, 'Jo came to London and she said: "How do you feel about sequels? Because I want them to grow up". She had it all worked out already. I said: "Let's take one book at a time "' (Steafel, 2016). This kind of forward planning certainly would have helped increase Rowling's chances of being adapted to other media platforms: it announces a storyworld that aims to continue, and develop, into the future.

Scholastic, a major US educational publisher, bought the US rights the same year for $105,000 and published the novel in America in October 1998 under the altered title *Harry Potter and the Sorcerer's Stone* and with minor adjustments to some English words. This was, in a certain precise sense, the novel's *first* adaptation. Arthur A. Levine, Scholastic's publisher, thought the word 'philosopher' was too 'arcane'; even so, he loved the book and managed to get an 'exceptional' first print run of 35,000 copies for it (Errington, 2017, p. 99). By 2000 the novel (and the two sequels) had been at the top of the *New York Times* bestseller list for long enough to make the newspaper decide to create a separate children's bestseller list to give competing adult novelists a break. 'The time has come', the *New York Times*' Book Review editor Charles McGrath declared, 'to clear some room' (Smith, 2000). Copies of the limited UK first edition soon became incredibly valuable. In his remarkably detailed, author-sanctioned, Bloomsbury-published bibliography of J. K. Rowling's work, Philip W. Errington reports that the auction record (by 2017) for a copy of the first edition of *Harry Potter and the Philosopher's Stone* was £57,000; he also notes that a first edition with the author's annotations and illustrations had sold a few years earlier for £150,000 to a private collector, who then immediately loaned the book to Oxford's Bodleian Library for its 2013 exhibition 'Magical Books: From the Middle Ages to Middle-Earth' (Errington, 2017, p. 4) – a book- and manuscript-based event built around the work of Oxford-educated fantasy authors like Tolkien. (Rowling is exceptional in another way here: she applied to Oxford but was not accepted, going instead to Exeter for her degree.) A variety of editions followed the initial *Harry Potter* publications: mass-market editions, 'deluxe' editions, 'school market' editions, 'house' editions. It is often noted that Rowling's novels were routinely split into those directly marketed to children and those marketed to adults. Among other things, this meant different cover art by different artists. Different editions also required new cover designs in order to appear distinctive. Bloomsbury's Harry Potter website lists six contributing artists (https://harrypotter.bloomsbury.com/uk/fun-stuff/meet-the-illustrators/), but there are others – for example, Mary GrandPré, who designed the covers and did chapter illustrations for all the novels published by Scholastic in the United States. Among other things, GrandPré invented the Harry Potter 'logo', 'where the letters seem to be formed from lightning bolts – a typographical motif that's since been used for the movies and virtually every piece of marketing for the series' (Shamsian, 2018). This illustrated signature became a key icon in the franchise storytelling afterlife of the novels.

The second novel, *Harry Potter and the Chamber of Secrets*, was first published in July 1998 in the United Kingdom and June 1999 in the United States. The third, *Harry Potter and the Prisoner of Azkaban*, was published in July 1999 in the United Kingdom and September 1999 in the United States; it was the fastest-selling book in that year, by the end of which the first three novels in the series had sold around 7.5 million copies (Miller, 1999). Rowling toured the United States in late 1999 when 'Pottermania' was well underway. In the meantime, the gaps between UK and US release dates were closing. The fourth novel, *Harry Potter and the Goblet of Fire*, was the first in the series to be released simultaneously in the United Kingdom and the United States, in June 2000. In the United Kingdom, it was launched at King's Cross Station in London, where there is now a *Platform 9¾* sign on the station concourse next to a Harry Potter merchandise shop. The last three novels in the series – *Harry Potter and the Order of the Phoenix* (2003), *Harry Potter and the Half-Blood Prince* (2005) and *Harry Potter and the Deathly Hallows* (2007) – were each given simultaneous global Anglophone release dates, with a myriad of translated versions to follow in languages from across the world, including Latin and Greek and even Lowland Scots ('Translatit intae Scots by Matthew Fitt'; the opening chapter of *Harry Potter and the Philosopher's Stone* is retitled 'The Laddie Wha Lived'). Dates of release were synchronised right down to an exact time: one minute past midnight on the winter solstice. Bloomsbury warned that bookshops breaking the embargos or leaking information to the media would never stock *Harry Potter* novels again.

The sales of these novels were phenomenal and record-breaking; even pre-release sales were in the millions. With each new novel, sales also increased. The *Half-Blood Prince* is reported to have sold 6.9 million copies in the United States in the first 24 hours of publication. In its first 24 hours in the United States, *Deathly Hallows* sold 8.3 million; by this time, the other six novels had sold around 325 million copies worldwide (Rich, 2007b). Very early in *Harry Potter and the Philosopher's Stone*, Professor McGonagall predicts that Potter will 'be famous – a legend . . . there will be books written about Harry – every child in our world will know his name!' (Rowling, 2013, p. 14). It is a confident author who can advocate the global popularity of her character right at the beginning of the first novel in a series that had only just begun. Twenty years later, in February 2018, J. K. Rowling's *Pottermore* website announced that half a billion *Harry Potter* novels had now been sold, with the series translated into 80 different languages. 'And the Harry Potter books are continuously evolving', the site adds, 'through new translations, gorgeous collectible editions, new jacket art, and new internal illustrations by renowned artists, who make us see our favourite characters in a new way' (Pottermore News Team, 2018). This is storytelling as a potentially endless process – corporate, collaborative and constantly active in the ongoing global reproduction, promotion and reconfiguration of the Harry Potter brand.

The adaptation of the *Harry Potter* novels to other media platforms began not long after the publication of *Philosopher's Stone*, when Bloomsbury began to produce audiobooks of the novels in the United Kingdom, read by Stephen Fry. In the United States, the Listening Library (then an independent company, now owned by Random House) acquired the audiobook rights to *Philosopher's Stone* in 1999 for $15,000, employing the British actor and former pop singer Jim Dale to do the readings. By the time Dale recorded *Deathly Hallows* in 2007, total audiobook sales in the United States were at almost six million. 'To create the range of voices', a *New York Times* article tells us, Dale called 'on his knowledge of dozens of accents from across the British Isles. . . . But it is his role as the aural embodiment of Harry Potter that has brought [him] a chance at the kind of immortality that many performers crave'. Dale put himself into a rich genealogy of fantasy adaptations and franchises: 'We have been part of history – big, big history', he remarked. 'It's like the people who were connected with Lewis Carroll or the people connected with J. M. Barrie when *Peter Pan* came up. It has been marvellous' (Rich, 2007a).

The question of who would become the 'embodiment' of Harry Potter became especially crucial to the film adaptations of the novels. In 1999 Rowling sold the film and worldwide merchandising rights to the first four novels to Warner Bros. for £1 million, with the stipulation that the principal cast be British. But a range of American directors were put forward, including Steven Spielberg, who wanted to make an animation that combined the first two novels, using the voice of an American child actor, Haley Joel Osment, for Potter. Warner Bros. finally hired the American director Chris Columbus and scriptwriter Steve Kloves. Columbus himself had another American child actor in mind for Potter. But several hundred boys later auditioned for the part after a general call for British-only Potter 'lookalikes', and finally Daniel Radcliffe was given the role. At the time Radcliffe was best known for playing the young David Copperfield in a BBC adaptation of Dickens's novel screened in the United Kingdom at the end of 1999: his Dickensian link may have been important here, with Dickens as a palpable influence on both Rowling's series and the films themselves (Groves, 2017, pp. 149–50).

Radcliffe was eleven years old when he got the part of Potter in *Harry Potter and the Philosopher's Stone* (or *Sorcerer's Stone* in the United States), released in November 2001 roughly midway between Rowling's fourth and fifth novel. Filming took place at Leavesden Studio, Hertfordshire, which had recently provided the set location for the Star Wars film *The Phantom Menace* (1999). All the *Harry Potter* films were made at Leavesden; Warner Bros. later purchased the studio in 2010, setting up a permanent tourist exhibition, 'Warner Bros. Studio Tour London – The Making of *Harry Potter*', to showcase the sets, props, costumes, models and drawings, special effects and so on. This is storyworld afterlife as a form of commemoration or homage to what is now a significant historical moment in global cinema. But it also demonstrates an interesting, perhaps unevenly balanced, collaborative relationship between US and UK companies in the wake of Rowling's sale of the film rights to her novels. A range of British heritage sites were drawn on in the making of the *Harry Potter* films, and many of them now have their own *Harry Potter* imprints: Gloucester Cathedral, for example, which has a '*Harry Potter* trail', or the Bodleian Library's Divinity School (which became the Hogwarts' Infirmary) and Duke Humfrey's Library (the Hogwart's Library's Restricted Section) in Oxford. This certainly suggests that the Harry Potter brand is also a British heritage brand. But American financial and directorial investment in all this complicates the picture and leaves its own imprint on British 'Pottermania'. This is no doubt partly why Hugh Grant, in his role as British Prime Minister in the popular film *Love, Actually* (2003) – coming in the wake of Columbus's 2001 film – is made to reprimand the American president for so casually taking US influence over Britain for granted: 'We may be a small country, but we're a great one too. The country of Shakespeare, Churchill, the Beatles, Sean Connery, Harry Potter'.

Columbus's *Harry Potter and the Sorcerer's Stone* went on to become the highest-grossing film of 2001, earning around $975 million worldwide. The remaining films-of-the-novels in the series were released in 2002, 2004, 2005, 2007, 2009 and – with the last novel, *Harry Potter and the Deathly Hollows*, split into two separate parts – 2010 and 2011. Each film earned a remarkable amount of money. The two films of the last novel doubled the worldwide gross earnings for Warner Bros.: $960 million for part 1 and more than $1.3 billion for part 2, making the latter the highest grossing film for 2011 and the highest-grossing film in the series. We can certainly feel overwhelmed by the scale of the financial investments and rewards in the

Harry Potter franchise. But it is also worth remembering that these films were creative projects too. They gathered together a large ensemble cast made up of highly-regarded actors (Emma Thompson, Gary Oldman, Maggie Smith, Alan Rickman, Ralph Fiennes, Kenneth Branagh, Helena Bonham-Carter, etc.) and amateurs who had little or no previous experience, like Rupert Grint (Ron Weasley) or the Irish actor Evanna Lynch (Luna Lovegood). Rowling had apparently wanted the Scottish actor Robbie Coltrane to play Hagrid; the producers had to turn down Robin Williams, who was keen to take the role. The films radiated a luscious, dark 'Gothic' look, helped by signature plumes of thin black smoke. Art direction and the generation of special effects had to seamlessly coexist. The renowned British production designer Stuart Craig helped create the visual world of Harry Potter during the ten years of its cinematic production. The sets, he has said, required a more 'theatrical, operatic' scale than the novels could suggest, although he also notes the films' fidelity to Rowling's work (Hanel, 2012). In an interview with *Architectural Digest*, Craig makes the interesting point that – because this was a film series built around shared locations – sets and materials could be 'recycled and reused'; at the end of it all, the films had effectively created their own 'archive of things' (Stamp, 2011). Just as importantly, as the films went on the budgets increased: so special effects could get better. A giant miniature model of Hogwarts would later become a digital model. A significant number of companies were involved in special effects or computer animation sequences: British companies such as Double Negative (or DNEG), Framestore (which created Dobby the house-elf, among other things), Baseblack (which did the ployjuice potion sequence) and Cinesite (which looked after Voldemort's nose), and the Australian company Rising Sun Pictures (which, for example, upgraded the Dementors for *Deathly Hallows, Part 1*). Creatures, prosthetics, makeup, costumes, music and soundtracks: these and many other things all play crucial parts in articulating the visual and aural atmospherics of film. In fantasy films, these things can seem to have extraordinary freedoms and the investment in them is considerable. On the other hand, they are also constrained, and influenced, by the designs and special effects that have preceded them. The British makeup effects and creature designer Nick Dudman has noted, for example, that designing dragons for the *Harry Potter* films meant producing recognisably generic creatures while trying to 'make them not look like what anyone else has done (before)' (Wilkin, 2012). Think of the white Gringott's dragon, for example, and compare it with Smaug in Peter Jackson's 2013 *Hobbit* film; think also of the dragons in the *Game of Throne* series, which I will comment on in Section 5.

The steady, sometimes staggered, release of the *Harry Potter* films over an extended period of time, coupled with the massive box office earnings, afforded Warner Bros. the opportunity to invest in further adaptations along the way. In 2000, just before the release of *Harry Potter and the Sorcerer's Stone*, Warner Bros.' parent company, Time Warner, merged with America Online Inc (AOL), resulting in a $350 billion corporation with links to almost every kind of media platform. This was a new kind of mega-merger, although it proved to be unstable and short-lived. Even so, the early *Harry Potter* films became crucial to AOL Time Warner's multi-media investment future. As Richard Parsons, its co-chief operating officer at the time, remarked, 'We use the different platforms to drive the movie, and the movie to drive business across the platforms' (Goff, 2006, p. 35). This is the corporate language of franchise storytelling. Simone Murray has rightly called the first *Harry Potter* film 'an indispensable brand anchor' for AOL Time Warner, the basis for a form of franchise development that saw 'subsequent content recycling and cross-promotion . . . structured to radiate outwards from this commercial epicentre' (Murray, 2002).

The films as a whole provided what is sometimes referred to as a 'golden age' for Warner Bros., and it certainly intended to capitalise on them. Warner Bros. went on to create a Harry Potter Global Franchise Development (HPGFD) team to manage the franchise, headed by Josh Berger: its aim was to 'develop and execute a high-level strategic vision for the Harry Potter brand and its ancillary businesses, working closely with J. K. Rowling's team at The Blair Partnership and other internal and external stakeholders and partners' (Eyre, 2014). Neil Blair was a former Warner Bros. executive; his literary and talent agency Blair Partnership took Rowling as its most prominent client, representing and protecting her interests in order to 'constantly grow one of the world's major entertainment franchises' (www.theblairpartnership.com/about/). A large number of franchise deals were done during this time – for example, with Coca-

Cola, which signed a £103 million deal to be the sole global marketing partner of *Harry Potter and the Sorcerer's Stone* (the film itself cost around £110 million to produce). J. K. Rowling was reported to have been reluctant to allow her character 'to be turned into a spokesman for Coca-Cola'. A company marketing executive, on the other hand, thought they were a perfect match: 'Both Harry Potter and Coca-Cola reach deep into the heart of local communities around the world', he said, 'to add a little bit of magic to people's everyday lives' (Day, 2001). Lucrative deals were also done with Mattel toys and LEGO. Then, in 2007, Universal Creative gained a licence from Warner Bros. to design *The Wizarding World of Harry Potter* theme park at the Universal Orlando Resort in Florida – with rides, a Hogwarts Express, a recreated Diagon Alley and even a Gringotts Money Exchange, where American dollars can be exchanged for Wizarding bank notes to buy gifts, wands and sweets. There are now two more Wizarding World theme parks at Universal Studios Japan and Universal Studios Hollywood. Pretty much every name, place or creature from the novels are now trademarked as a licensed brand – the most prominent of these is, of course, Harry Potter™.

Writing in 2006, Patricia M. Goff commented in the transformation of a fantasy character into a brand and a franchise:

> Harry Potter is well on its way to becoming one of the most beloved stories of this generation. The series is, for the most part, viewed as a positive development in the life of the contemporary adolescent, firing her imagination and awakening the reader within. So does it matter if Time Warner also benefits? Does it matter if Harry Potter emerges from a media landscape increasingly characterised by fewer, bigger conglomerates, the marriage of content and delivery, and the exploitation of the most popular brand properties across multiple media outlets? The short answer is, 'it might'. (Goff, 2006, p. 37)

The transmedia adaptation of fantasy novels by writers like Tolkien and Rowling came at a time when media entertainment conglomerates got bigger and could invest more in their product. But I have also argued that modern fantasy – by the 1950s and beyond – was already receptive to these developments, working towards a cultural logic of scale or magnitude through the steady, continual production of extended sequences of (often very long, elaborate) novels. Media entertainment conglomerates like Warner Bros. are then obliged to respond to the requirements of scale not just in terms of deals, negotiations and investments, but also in terms of *creativity*. Outsourcing to smaller companies like Double Negative or Framestore and employing design teams like those overseen by Nick Dudman are one way of coping with, distributing and co-ordinating scale: it has to be a matter of collaboration between creative partners.

As I have noted, the modern fantasy genre pushes itself towards world-building magnitude and continuous production, as if its elaborately-orchestrated project is always yet to be completed. It routinely adds to its own oeuvre with prequels and sequels, often massively extending its range, its genealogies, its narratives and sub-narratives. Certainly what is often called the Potterverse shows no signs of coming to an end. In 2001 Rowling published a 'guidebook' called *Fantastic Beasts and Where to Find Them*, under the penname of Newt Scamander, a wizard who had attended Hogwarts many years ago and went on to work at the Ministry of Magic. *Fantastic Beasts* is a school textbook mentioned (and consulted) occasion-ally in the *Harry Potter* novels, supposedly written by Scamander in 1927. Rowling's 2001 publication has a foreword written by 'Albus Dumbledore' that legitimates her book as an official part of the franchise and brazenly urges readers to buy it: 'I was deeply honoured when Newt Scamander asked me to write the foreword for this very special edition of *Fantastic Beasts and Where to Find Them*. Newt's masterpiece has been an approved textbook at Hogwart's School of Witchcraft and Wizardry ever since its publication … yet it is not a book to be confined to the classroom. No wizarding household is complete without a copy of *Fantastic Beasts*' (Rowling, 2001, p. xiii). Twelve years later, Rowling and Warner Bros. announced plans to develop a series of films based on her *Fantastic Beasts* book, with screenplays by Rowling herself. They would form a set of prequels to the Harry Potter story. The first film in the series, *Fantastic Beasts and Where to Find Them*, directed by David Yates, was released

2016, costing around $180 million to produce and with gross earnings of around $814 million worldwide. In an interview with *Entertainment Weekly*, Rowling talked about Scamander's enemy, the dark wizard Grindelwald, as 'part of the canon from the beginning' and 'essential to an understanding of how Dumbledore became Dumbledore' (Rankin, 2018). This is a fantasy author working to legitimate or normalise (or 'canonise') subsequent narrative digressions. Her comments on the prequel series recall her meeting with Bloomsbury more than twenty years earlier when she pitched the *Harry Potter* novels ('How do you feel about sequels?'): 'As with the *Harry Potter* books, it is all mapped out. In fact, when we announced the five films, I talked about that. It's always possible that some details will change along the way, but the arc of the story is there. It's been an amazing opportunity to tell parts of the backstory that never made it into the original books' (Rankin, 2018). Modern fantasy in this account steadily releases parts of its own prehistory and turns them into a storyworld afterlife that enthusiastically crosses over into other media platforms.

Rowling's 2001 edition of *Fantastic Beasts* was republished after the film in 2017, with additional content and new artwork by Jonny Duddle (who had also illustrated some *Harry Potter* children's editions) and the Croatian artist Tomislav Tomic. She also published her original screenplay of Yates's film in a 2018 book that included a glossary of film terms (jump cut, montage, etc.) and took the opportunity to promote her *Pottermore* website, 'the digital heart of the Wizarding World'. The name *Pottermore* does indeed suggest that one can never have enough of Rowling's 'Potterverse', and the website certainly overflows with promotional commentary, news about events, games, e-commerce and ebook opportunities, ephemera, and tidbits of exclusive material. Rowling's primary commercial partner here was Sony, which helped set up the website in 2012 (although the partnership ended a few year later). The site is a way of re-establishing Rowling's authority over the Potterverse after so much outsourcing and transmedia storytelling. It also seamlessly links the role of the author with her capacity to promote and sell products. But *Pottermore* also wanted to interact with, and attract, Potterverse fans. In an interview with *Bookseller*, Charlie Radmayne, the

CEO at *Pottermore*, captured the often-hidden connections between expanding the fan base, promoting brands and protecting licences:

> What we've done with *Pottermore* is harness a fanbase of millions of the biggest *Harry Potter* fans. In terms of producing value to all of the rights holders – be it J. K. Rowling, Bloomsbury, Scholastic, Warner Bros, or indeed our sponsor Sony – that's an immensely valuable thing as any new books, content or products come out. . . . What we will be shaping out now is how to engage with new fans. . . . So there will be more interactivity, more community books – this is critical for us if we are to engage with these new fans. (Missingham, 2012)

Pottermore is literally about getting more Potter fans – but within the framework of an already heavily regulated corporate brand ownership.

The fantasy genre can attract significant fan activity, often to do with quasi-official activities like providing information about characters, events, genealogies, plot details and so on. Some of these, like *The Leaky Cauldron*, are on good terms with Rowling and Warner Bros.; *The Leaky Cauldron's* webmistress, Melissa Anelli, is also a consultant for *Pottermore* and author of *Harry: A History* (2008), for which Rowling wrote an approving, authorising foreword. But other kinds of fan activity can run into difficulty. Fan fiction or *fanfic*, for example, can take *Harry Potter* narratives in a range of unanticipated directions; it is an unauthorised, amateur form of creative adaptation. Warner Bros. has been especially punishing as far as unauthorised fan activity is concerned, determined to protect the brand in which it has invested so much. In 2001 Heather Lawver Sewell set up her *Daily Prophet* website, a 'participatory communication environment' (Gupta, 2009, p. 221). It was around this time that Warner Bros. began to serve fan sites with 'cease-and-desist' orders. Lawver Sewell responded by setting up a Defence Against the Dark Arts (DADA) campaign; in the United Kingdom, Alastair Aexander set up PotterWar.org.uk; and soon, protests against the heavy-handedness of Warner Bros. were underway, which saw the company back down and become (rhetorically, at least) more accommodating to amateur fan activity.

But a number of subsequent lawsuits over intellectual property played themselves out. In October 2007 Warner Bros. and Rowling filed a copyright suit against RDR Books in the United States, which wanted to publish a major reference work by Steve Vander Ark, a Michigan librarian, titled the *Harry Potter Lexicon*. The *Lexicon* already existed online as an unofficial Harry Potter fansite, but Rowling had her own plans to publish a Potter encyclopaedia in book form. In the event, an abridged, unauthorised version of the *Lexicon* was finally published, and a new online *Harry Potter Lexicon* was launched, with Rowling's blessing: she wrote on *Pottermore* in July 2016, 'I had the privilege of being part of this, collaborating with the visual aspect of this new Harry Potter encyclopaedia'. The difference between a lawsuit and a collaboration can indeed sometimes be difficult to determine. More recently – as a final example of litigation against fan adaptations or spin-offs of source texts – an Italian director, Gianmaria Pezzato, made an English-language film titled *Voldemort: Origins of the Heir*, uploaded to YouTube in early 2018. It is an excellent film, an unofficial prequel to the *Harry Potter* films – tracking the transition from Tom Riddle to Voldemort – that raised its production money through crowdsourcing. But Warner Bros. intervened and shut the crowdsourcing down. Finally, they agreed to let the film proceed as a nonprofit venture, affirming its status as an amateur project. In this and other cases of fan-based adaptations, it can also be difficult to determine whether an unofficial spin-off is a narrative deviation from the official canon or a homage to that canon.

There is view among some commentators – and fans – that Rowling's Harry Potter franchise is in any case producing too much and saying too much (e.g., Wahlquist, 2019). But it does seem to keep on going, potentially, at least, without end. *Harry Potter and the Cursed Child* is a stage play based on an original story that saw Rowling collaborate with British playwright Jack Thorne and theatre director John Tiffany. It developed out of the epilogue to *Deathly Hallows*, Rowling's last novel in the series, where the characters, now grown up, are sending their own children off to Hogwarts. The play opened in New York in April 2018; productions in London and Melbourne soon followed. The *New York Times* called it 'the most expensive Broadway nonmusical play ever', costing around $68.5 million to produce (Paulson, 2018); it was performed in two parts, and ran for five and a half hours. Scale or magnitude remain crucial to authorised Harry Potter adaptations, much as they did with Tolkien. Interestingly, the casting of actors became a key issue, a way of addressing (to a degree, at least) what the *Harry Potter* novels and films, with their three white child protagonists, had never directly considered: ethnic diversity. For the London production, black actor Noma Dumezweni was cast as Hermione Granger; her casting enabled belated, critical readings of race in Rowling's novels (e.g., Berlatsky, 2015). In Melbourne, Hermione was played by the African Australian actor, Paula Arundell. We have already seen examples of how transmedia storytelling can work to reconfigure what an earlier original creative work might have taken for granted – for better or worse, depending on the case. In visual and performative media platforms like theatre and cinema, the generic whiteness of fantasy can be adjusted and even remade – this is something the Potterverse is still getting used to.

5 George R. R. Martin and HBO's *Game of Thrones*

George R. R. Martin shares the same middle initials as J. R. R. Tolkien, although this is of course a coincidence. Even so, Martin was once called 'the American Tolkien' in *Time Magazine* in 2005, after the publication of the fourth novel in his *A Song of Ice and Fire* series, *A Feast for Crows* (and six years before the first season of the HBO television adaptation, *A Game of Thrones*). The novel's reviewer, Lev Grossman, noted some comparisons between the two writers but drew some important distinctions as well:

> Martin has produced – is producing, since the series isn't over – the great fantasy epic of our era. It's an epic for a more profane, more jaded, more ambivalent age than the one Tolkien lived in. Tolkien was a veteran of the Somme, and *The Lord of the Rings* was partly written during World War II. . . . Tolkien wrote at a time when it really seemed as if a war was on for the fate of civilization.
>
> Now we're not even sure what civilization is. (Grossman, 2011)

Martin was a successful fantasy and SF writer before he began *A Song of Ice and Fire*, publishing work that has been nominated for the Hugo and Locus Awards and the World Fantasy Award. His novel *Dying of the Light* (1977) is in the SF Masterworks series, and his American vampire novel *Fevre Dream* (1982) is in the Fantasy Masterworks series. He has often published collaboratively and is an inveterate anthologiser with the *Wild Cards* and *Dangerous Women* series; the first volume of the latter (2013) included Martin's story 'The Princess and the Queen', chronicling the defeat and death of Rhaenyra Targaryen. He had also written for television, less successfully. *A Song of Ice and Fire* began in 1996 with the first novel, *A Game of Thrones*: the beginning of a projected series of at least seven novels of bleak, violent high fantasy, sometimes known as 'grimdark'. It is also a medievalist fantasy, drawing on the War of the Roses (1455–87), with House Lannister obviously recalling the House of Lancaster. Martin took the novelist and historian Thomas B. Costain's four volume *Plantagenets* series (1949–62) as a 'model' for his modern fantasy series: 'It's old-fashioned history', he has said in an interview; '[Costain is] not interested in analysing socioeconomic trends or cultural shifts so much as the wars and the assignations and the murders and the plots and the betrayals, all the juicy stuff' (Flood, 2018). *A Clash of Kings* followed *A Game of Thrones* in 1998; *A Storm of Swords* in 2000; *A Feast for Crows* in 2005; and *A Dance with Dragons* in 2011. Sales of the novels began slowly but grew steadily; by the time of *A Dance with Dragons*, the series had sold around twelve million copies worldwide (Whitehead, 2018). But publication dates grew further apart with the fourth and fifth novels, and as I write the last two books in Martin's projected series, *The Winds of Winter* and *A Dream of Spring*, have yet to be completed. Interestingly, instead of finishing *The Winds of Winter*, Martin went on to publish the first, long volume of projected prequel to *A Song of Ice and Fire*, titled *Fire and Blood* (2018), which chronicles the rise of the Targaryen dynasty in Westeros. The production of a lengthy prequel set during a much earlier time might recall Tolkien's *Silmarillion*; Martin has in fact referred to the project as his 'GRRM-arillion' (Hibberd, 2018), which also references the 'grimdark' fantasy subgenre.

David Benioff and D. B. Weiss had met at Trinity College, Dublin, two graduate students from the United States 'obsessed with Irish literature' (Windolf, 2014); Benioff went on to write a thesis on Samuel Beckett while Weiss's thesis was on James Joyce's *Finnegans Wake* (1939). Later, back in the United States, they had some success as novelists and screenplay writers. In 2005 they read Martin's first four novels and thought about the possibility of adapting the series. They had a long lunch with Martin to discuss the project; Martin asked them a question about his novels ('Who is Jon Snow's real mother?'), and he was apparently impressed with their answer. Benioff and Weiss then pitched the project to HBO, which bought the television rights in 2007. They initially made a 'shoddy pilot' (Windolf, 2014) but were in any case given the green light to go ahead, with a commitment from HBO for a budget of $50 million and a full season of ten episodes, seven of which were written by Benioff and Weiss; episode eight was written by Martin himself. The principal cast were mostly British and Irish actors, some experienced (like Sean Bean or Charles Dance) and some who were relatively new to the profession. Season one was filmed in 2010 and premiered on HBO on 17 April 2011, with an audience of around 2.5 million in the United States, not especially large but significant enough. (Audiences – legitimate and otherwise – would grow quickly as the seasons progressed.) The first episode famously opened with Ned Stark's child, Bran, being asked to not to look away as his father decapitates a deserter. The *Game of Thrones* series immediately announced itself (as did Martin's novels) as *adult* fantasy, quite different to Tolkien's *The Hobbit* and *The Lord of the Rings* or Rowling's *Harry Potter* novels. Children might also watch, but – like Ned Stark with Bran – that would be determined by the adults in the room. It seemed perfectly suited to HBO.

Home Box Office, Inc., is the oldest operating pay television service in the United States, launched in November 1972 by the cable entrepreneur Chuck Dolan. It is now a division of WarnerMedia. By the mid-1990s HBO was increasingly producing its own made-for-television programs, presenting a range of often long-running adult-oriented drama series that gained critical acclaim – notably, *The Sopranos* (1999–2007), *Six Feet Under* (2001–5), *Deadwood* (2004–6), *The Wire* (2002–8), *Rome* (2005–7) and *True Blood* (2008–14). These kinds of programs are often called 'long-form television': highly stylised 'quality' television that generates complex and long-lasting serial narratives, with provocative themes and charismatic central characters. Drawing on the work of Pierre Bourdieu, Christopher Anderson has suggested that HBO since *The Sopranos* has been building an 'aristocratic disposition' of taste in its television audiences, creating 'a luxury brand in a populist medium' (Anderson, 2013, pp. 25, 30). It has ushered in one of the 'golden ages' of television, expanding acceptable content and making a commitment to a complexity of character development and narrative not usually seen outside of cinema. For Martin, cinema itself would have not been able adequately to adapt the multi-narrative arcs of his long, meandering novels: 'It took Peter Jackson three movies to make Tolkien's *Lord of the Rings*, and he still had to cut things', he said in an interview; 'It would take three movies for *A Storm of Swords* alone!' (Seale, 2015). The problem here is whether screen adaptation could do justice to the scale of the novels themselves. Martin certainly didn't object to the adaptation of his series, but he 'always thought they were unfilmable' (Brown, 2014): too many characters, too many episodes, too many narrative threads. Cinema people, he remarked, wanted to reduce these things to a central story about one principal character:

> [T]hey said, "Well, yes, it's true, it's too complex; it's too big the way it is – but we have to find the central arc. And we've decided the central arc should be Jon Snow". So the whole movie would be about Jon Snow. "Or the central arc is Daenerys. The whole movie would be about this exiled princess, and she gives birth to dragons". That might be a good movie, and it might be interesting, but it wouldn't be my story. My story is a combination of stuff. (Brown, 2014)

Filming the novels in Martin's series certainly required long-form television already to exist; it also required large-scale investment over an extended period of time, with all eight seasons running from 2011 to 2019. Each season has been more expensive than the previous one as the cast has grown and the battles have become bigger. By the sixth season (2016), episodes were costing around $10 million each to produce. The final six episodes of the last season, season eight (2019), reportedly cost more than $15 million each. Battle scenes are especially expensive to film. In season one, Tyrion is knocked unconscious early on during the Battle of the Green Fork and when he wakes up, the battle is over: there simply wasn't enough money to stage the event itself. The Battle of Blackwater Bay in season two was a different matter. Benioff and Weiss wanted to stage it, but it was difficult to negotiate for more money to do so. In an interview, Benioff has said:

> For budgetary reasons, we came very, very close to having all the action take place off-screen, the way plays have handled battle scenes for a few thousand years. The idea was that we'd set most of the episode in Maegor's Holdfast. Cersei and Sansa would be cooped up in there with the other noblewomen and children, hearing occasional reports from the battlements. Last year we had to cut a battle we wanted to shoot, and the Battle of Blackwater Bay is far more

important. To our minds, the entire season builds to this clash, and if we didn't see any of it, we were undercutting the story and short-changing the audience. (Robinson, 2017)

The episode cost $8 million to produce. Later battles became larger and even more expensive. The Battle of the Bastards in episode nine, season six, took twenty-five days to film (in Northern Ireland), requiring six hundred crew members, five hundred extras, seventy horses and riders, and sixty-five stunt people (Hibberd, 2016). The gruelling episode gained critical acclaim and won seven Emmys; the director, Miguel Sapochnik, is supposed to have been influenced by Akira Kurosawa's epic period drama *Ran* (1985) – at the time, the most expensive Japanese film in history – for the battle scene's elaborate, point-of-view choreography. Unsurprisingly, the concluding battle in season eight – the Battle of Winterfell – increased the magnitude still further, as 'the longest consecutive battle ever committed to film', larger in scale than the Battle of Helm's Deep in the second of Peter Jackson's *The Lord of the Rings* films, *The Two Towers* (Hibberd, 2019).

I have suggested in this book that the adaptation of modern fantasy, to cinema and television in particular, requires long-term commitment and the capacity to provide large-scale, continuously increasing investment, film by film or season by season. So the media entertainment corporations behind modern fantasy's adaptations must themselves be large-scale. Producers must be able to assemble (and afford) the various component parts that enable scale or magnitude to happen – to realise modern fantasy's epic aspirations. But details are important, too, especially in a narrative that is broken into so many different threads and where changes in a character's fortunes can happen so quickly. The creation of scenes and events, costumes, creatures and exterior and interior sets can turn on the smallest of details. Costume designer Michelle Clayton has spoken about the women characters' costumes in season seven, as Sansa, Cersei and Daenerys become more powerful: 'At this stage, everything has reached such a zenith in their character development that everything they do and say symbolically means something. Even Dany's rings, her jewellery – every single bit says something about the character. From the brittleness of the glass on Cersei and the metal rings on Dany and the way that now others are wearing things to show their allegiance' (Renfro, 2017). This is not mass production; it is skilled craft work and artisanal labour, not all that far away from Willian Morris and Co.'s textile art. Colour, texture, volume, surface, ornamentation, symbols: these things work to give precision to a character's mood and predicament, which change and develop as the seasons progress. Other things also develop: like the three dragons, Drogon, Viserion and Rhaegal. The design of the dragons in *Game of Thrones* changed markedly, from their beginnings as newborns to their fully fledged adulthood and (in one case) zombie afterlife. The chief designer was Emmy Award–winning Dan Katcher, the so-called father of dragons. But a number of visual effects studios were also involved: the London-based Bluebolt, for example, for the baby dragons, and the German company Pixomondo as the dragons became larger. Sven Martin, Pixomondo's visual effects supervisor, worked with a team of artists to produce both scale (literally) and micro-detail, basing designs on actual creatures, such as lizards, bats and chickens: 'For the skin color patterns we went even further, picking ideas from frogs or cheetahs', Martin has said; 'Every detail of the dragons has a counterpart in the animal world' (Cooper, 2019).

It is not just design that is important to the details of these particular screen adaptations. Like Tolkien's *The Lord of the Rings*, Martin's *A Song of Ice and Fire* created new words in invented languages, like Dothraki or Valyrian. But neither of these languages are well developed in the novels. The HBO producers employed the US linguist David J. Peterson to develop a more extensive spoken language for the adaptations, creating more than three thousand new words. 'I started with the material from *A Song of Ice and Fire*, and then tried to build out the language around that', Peterson has said.

> I tried to imagine the circumstances of the Dothraki people, and that, combined with what I know about pre-industrialized languages and cultures, helped to determine what the language should look like, what vocabulary would be appropriate (what would be native, what would be derived, etc.). . . . I tend to think of the sound as a mix between Arabic (minus the distinctive pharyngeals) and Spanish, due to the dental consonants. (Wright, 2010)

One of the spin-offs of the HBO series is Peterson's 'conversational language course' book, *Living Language: Dothraki* (2014): this invented language can be learned and shared, even though it is entirely internal to the *Game of Thrones* adaptations. Scenes, too, can have their own elaborate internal logic, tied to processes of adaptation that (like the Dothraki language) can turn out to be surprisingly idiosyncratic. One example is the so-called Dying Man or Beckett scene in episode seven, season four, when Arya and the Hound find a dying farmer and ask him why he doesn't put an end to his suffering. 'The thought has occurred to me', he says. 'So why go on?' Arya asks. 'Habit', he replies – after which there is a brief discussion about what 'nothing' is, referencing Clov and Hamm's discussion of nothing in Beckett's play, *Endgame* (1957). The farmer is played by Barry McGovern, an Irish actor well known for his one-man Beckett theatre performances. And of course, this connects back to David Benioff's thesis on Beckett while at Trinity College, Dublin: an idiosyncratic citational moment in the large-scale screen adaptation of a series of fantasy novels by a media entertainment corporation. We could even say that Beckett's play is itself adapted here, pulled into the reconfiguring frame of modern fantasy transmedia storytelling.

HBO's *Game of Thrones* is relatively unusual as far as transmedia adaptations are concerned because it outpaced Martin's series, which was still incomplete by 2019 when the HBO adaptation came to an end. This meant that the adaptation had to create its own narrative strands and make its own way towards a conclusion – although it is also supposed to have remained true to Martin's broad plan for his source texts. Season five (2015) had already begun to move beyond the last novel in *A Song of Ice and Fire*, killing off characters (like Shireen Baratheon, in one of the most brutal and heart-wrenching deaths of the adaptations) that were still alive in Martin's novels. By this time, as fan commentator Walt Hickey noted, we saw 'the end of the published arcs' of a number of major characters, including Cersei, Sansa, Tyrion, Daenerys and Jon Snow (Hickey, 2015). The close of season five saw an increasing split between fans of the novels and audiences of the HBO television series. By season six, the television series had left the former behind to create its own 'universe' of narrative and character development. It had become an 'off-book adaptation'. There was even a view that Martin's series was now superfluous because the television series had 'outgrown' it

(Dreyfuss, 2017). But commentators also noted that by season seven the pace had significantly increased (with characters often travelling incredibly long distances in the smallest amount of time) and the focus had intensified, moving away from multiple narrative threads to begin to bring the key strands of the series together. A once-meandering storyline became suddenly more efficient, reduced to one major, fundamental struggle rather than a criss-crossing sequence of battles, clashes, encounters and skirmishes. For Christopher Hooton, this was a negative: 'the show has let character fall by the wayside', he wrote; 'Interactions and revelations that would once have been parcelled out slowly now tend to get no more than a handful of terse sentences back and forth on a frosty battlement' (Hooton, 2018).

Martin himself had written one episode per season for *Game of Thrones*; but the last episode he wrote was for season four ('The Lion and the Rose') and it was significantly altered in production by Benioff and Weiss (Robinson, 2018). So the author shifted away from the television adaptations as they increasingly began to go their own way – although he remained in the role of an executive co-producer. The adaptation's departure from the source texts led to some criticism from those loyal to Martin's work – for example, that the 'strength' of Benioff and Weiss 'is in adaptation, not necessarily innovation'; 'the show is simply not as good as it was when it had Martin's books to guide it' (Tassi, 2018). The final season in 2019 drew especially intense levels of source-text fan resentment. Daenerys's rapid descent into vengeful madness and mass murder, along with Ayra's sudden, unexpected killing of the Night King when all seemed lost, were among the turn of events that contributed to a fan petition with 1.4. million signatures calling for Benioff and Weiss to remake all the episodes. *ThinkStory* founder Daniel Whidden released a sixteen-minute video to YouTube entitled 'How Game of Thrones Should Have Ended': he went back to the novels to look at different possibilities, different narrative threads (e.g., to do with the Children of the Forest) that might have played a more prominent role later on. Even commentators in the literary magazines seemed disappointed: for example, Andrew Irwin complained in the *Times Literary Supplement* about the way the 'vast ephemeral constellation of the possible' in HBO's *Game of Thrones* 'had to end with the dull thud of the determinate' (Irwin, 2019, p. 21). In the *London Review of*

Books, the novelist John Lanchester was more forgiving: although he admired 'the depth and density of the imagined world' of the novels and the earlier HBO seasons, he thought 'the writers knew what they were doing' in season eight (Lanchester, 2019, p. 16). A view that was more sympathetic to an adaptation's improvisational freedom tended to criticise 'the perpetually disappointed figure of the fan' who doggedly remains loyal to the source texts (Greenway, 2019). And of course, although it may have departed from the novels, the worldwide success of the HBO series, broadcast in 170 countries, in fact massively increased their sales and range: more than 85 million copies of the novels sold by 2018, translated into 47 languages (Yu, 2018).

In an interesting article in *Salon* – although perhaps it forgets about HBO's *True Blood* – Sonia Saraiya comments on how unusual it must once have seemed to get a modern adult fantasy series adapted for television by HBO: 'In 2011 it was difficult to imagine a prestige adult television series based on an unfinished set of fantasy novels published mostly in the late '90s. The *Harry Potter* and *Lord Of The Rings* books and movies were successful, but decidedly not sexy' (Saraiya, 2016). As she notes, *Game of Thrones* initially seemed 'revolutionary', self-consciously seeking to 'deconstruct the tropes of fantasy novels like *The Lord of the Rings* trilogy' (Saraiya, 2016), not least through its focus on the determined rise to power of female characters like Cersei, Daenerys, Arya and Sansa Stark. But the adult-oriented 'sexiness' of HBO's *Game of Thrones* became a problem, with its surplus of naked women, bare breasts and so on. Sex scenes either not in the novels or modified by the HBO adaptations sometimes seemed unnecessarily sadistic and brutal – for example, Joffrey Baratheon's torture and murder of prostitutes (one of whom, Ros, was invented for the television series) in season two, episode four; Ramsey Bolton's rape of Sansa Stark on their wedding night in season five, episode six, with Theon Greyjoy forced to watch; and Khal Drogo's wedding-night rape of Daenerys in the first episode of season one (their sex in Martin's novel is by contrast much gentler and respectful – with Drogo an apparent expert in the art of prolonged foreplay and Daenerys finally whispering her consent at the end of the scene; see Martin, 1996, p. 103). For Sansa and Deanerys especially, it seemed as if the HBO adaptation was suggesting that violent sex is a necessary way of ushering them into a 'knowing' kind of womanhood – an initiation into power to come. Many female viewers protested and complained; *Mary Sue*, a feminist online community of popular culture fans and 'geeks', refused to continue to promote *Game of Thrones* on its website; a US Democrat senator, Claire McCaskill, tweeted after the Sansa episode, 'I'm done with *Game of Thrones*'.

In another article on the HBO series, Saraiya offered a broader critique of the intensity of the violence staged on screen (burning bodies alive, crushing heads, decapitation, etc.), recognising that HBO viewers (those who pay to view, at least) are 'in the global 1 percent' (Saraiya, 2014). The 'thirst for blood' in HBO's *Game of Thrones*, she writes,

> has gotten in the way of *Thrones*' fundamental truth: a connection and reconnection to empathy and understanding, a lens that offers not just brutality, but also the assiduous follow-through of healing, grieving, and surviving. . . . It's a show that delights in showing the audience how easily our bodies can be destroyed. But it would do well to remember that there are some audience members who know all too well how fragile and mortal their own bodies can be. (Saraiya, 2014)

But the fragility of bodies is a theme in the HBO adaptation, already announced in that opening scene where Bran is told to not look away as a character (with whom we are asked to sympathise) is executed. What holds reader and viewer interest in *Game of Thrones* surely has much to do with the sheer mortality of characters, who might die abruptly and unexpectedly – and, in the case of someone like Ned Stark, are mourned for a considerable period of time, shaping the trajectories of other characters in the process. The variability of a character's fortunes in the series made narrative trajectories notoriously difficult to predict. Fan commentaries on the HBO series as it unfolded were thus often about speculation: what might happen next, what buried bits of narrative can help predict future trajectories. Fan activity or *fanac* can be remarkably busy here, providing guides to characters and events, information, promotional material – and encouraging even more speculation. Fan-based conventions (e.g., Comicon) gather these things together, bringing producers, cast members, technicians and sometimes Martin himself together for Q&A sessions. (Martin had apparently attended the very first Comicon in New York in July 1964.) Fanac built around the *Game of Thrones* series, as Charles Yu has put it, seemed to be 'in a permanent state of frenzy'; its often elaborate activities would not be possible 'with a lesser series, one without the complexity and consistency to support all of this geekery' (Yu, 2018). Fan-generated websites and blogs such as *A Wiki of Ice and Fire, Westeros.org, Watchersonthewall.com* and *Racefortheironthrone.wordpress.com* are often huge clearing houses for information and promotional material: they work in sync with the series (the 'canon') in a kind of self-validating loop. We have seen something similar with Harry Potter and Tolkien fan sites: these fantasy series similarly generate more than enough complexity to warrant the kind of curatorial care fans often enthusiastically bestow upon them. HBO's *Game of Thrones* may be part of a 'golden age' of television, but it has also produced what Caroline Siede calls 'the golden age of internet fandom'. 'Fandom', she writes, 'is no longer just a companion to the media it celebrates; it's become a form of entertainment in its own right. This is partially organic – the internet has always been good at community-building. But there is another, more practical reason that fandom has taken on a life of its own. As franchises become more and more complicated, casual fans are struggling keep up' (Siede, 2016). Fan websites, blogs and podcasts all do the work of transmedia or franchise storytelling precisely by trying not just to keep up but to get on top of it all, and to get ahead: providing information and news that can work to orient readers and viewers (and as we saw with Rowling, even authors) who want to increase their knowledge of the series to which they are committed for the long term. They enable us – should we want to pay attention to the things they do – to immerse ourselves more deeply and thoroughly into the elaborate *Game of Thrones* storyworld, which is why the last season, as it tried to bring the storyworld to a close, generated so much fan resentment.

The storyworld of Martin's *A Song of Ice and Fire* is, of course, still unfolding. This is because the canon itself is now a matter of franchise storytelling, which keeps on giving: more sequels, more prequels, more spin-offs and more merchandise. Various spin-off or 'companion' books include Martin's *The Wit and Wisdom of Tyrion Lannister* (2013), illustrated by Jonty Clark, and Martin's collaboration with two 'superfans', Elio M. Garcia Jr. and Linda Antonsson, *The World of Ice and Fire* (2014), with illustrations by Michael Komarck and Ted Nasmith – also well known as an illustrator of Tolkien's work. There is even an official *Game of Thrones* cookbook, Chelsea Monroe-Cassel and Sariann Lehrer's *A Feast of Ice and Fire* (2012), with an authorising foreword by Martin. *Game of Thrones* has developed its own games, too, and a wide range of collectibles, T-shirts, gifts and so on. With the US toy and board-game company Hasbro, Inc., HBO released a *Game of Thrones* version of *Monopoly* (2015, 2018), reminding players that the fantasy series is also about banking, trade, property ownership and the paying of debts. Different entertainment media platforms enable different ways of configuring – and experiencing – the stories of the franchise. At least a half dozen video games have been produced out of the *Game of Thrones* franchise, often also in licensed partnership with HBO. The US independent video-game studio Telltale Games – a *New York Times* article calls them the 'HBO of gaming' (Parker, 2014) – gained a licence from HBO to produce their own six-episode *Game of Thrones*, reportedly with Martin's personal assistant Ty Corey Franck as a story consultant. It is built around House Forrester (not in the HBO adaptation and mentioned in passing only in Martin's *A Dance with Dragons*), and it begins with the murders at the Red Wedding. There have also been touring exhibitions and 'live concert experiences' (www.gameofthronesconcert.com), once again authorised by HBO. These kinds of franchise-driven adaptations and spin-offs expand the experience of *Game of Thrones* storyworlds, working as (to recall the term I introduced in the opening section of this book) transmedia paratexts.

Just before the final season of the television adaptation of *Game of Thrones* screened in April to June 2019, HBO released a number of videos to YouTube of the actors commenting on their experience of working in a fantasy series for so many years. Younger actors like Maisie Williams (Arya) or Isaac Hempstead-Wright (Bran) had literally grown up with the adaptation, gaining confidence in their craft as the series went on. The cast spoke of themselves as a 'family'; they bonded as friends. In fact, during the course of the series, Kit Harrington (Jon Snow) and Rose Leslie (Ygritte), who had played lovers in the *Game of Thrones* series, were married in real life. Actors spoke of the experience of filming for so long – and often under rigorous conditions in remote locations, like Iceland – as something that had 'changed them forever'. Even so, they agreed that the HBO series finally and inevitably had to come to an end. But it didn't. In November 2018 Martin announced the beginning of the HBO production of a prequel to *Game of Thrones* with the provisional title *The Long Night*; casting got underway not long afterwards. Martin co-created the story, set thousands of years before the events in *Game of Thrones*, with the English author and screenwriter Jane Goldman (Otterson, 2019). I have suggested in this book that the modern fantasy genre has routinely worked by extending its own storyworlds into the future and back into the past, potentially without end. It relies on the creation of charismatic characters who function under duress, securing loyalties but also making enemies along the way, moving from one place to another, seeing new sights, learning new things. Modern fantasy calls those characters into action; it literally summons them, as Frodo is summoned by Gandalf in *The Lord of the Rings* or as Arya is summoned by Jaqen H'ghar in Martin's novels and the *Game of Thrones* television series. The secondary worlds it invents are densely populated, always contested, full of mystery and danger; the narratives it pursues take characters from landscape to landscape, event by event and episode by episode. These attributes all help make modern fantasy attractive to transmedia adaptation and, in a significant number of cases, franchise storytelling; but they also pose challenges because they require long-term investment and a sense of scale or magnitude that can do justice to the sheer expansiveness of the genre itself. In fact, as early as 2014 – at the opening of season four of HBO's *Game of Thrones* – Martin was already thinking about spin-offs and bigger budgets, hinting of the possibility of some films based on his *Tales of Dunk and Egg* novellas (1998, 2003, 2010), which unfold around ninety years before events in *A Song of Ice and Fire*. 'It all depends on how long the main series runs', he said; 'Do we run for seven years? Do we run for eight? Do we run for 10? The books get bigger and bigger (in scope). It might need a feature to tie things up, something with a feature budget, like $100 million for two hours. Those dragons get real big, you know' (Siegel, 2014). This is the exponential, 'epic' logic of the modern fantasy genre after 1955; its many transmedia adaptations have tended to escalate that logic into a multiplatform entertainment media franchise that, in the cases of Tolkien, Rowling and Martin, shows little sign of slowing down.

References

Anderson, C. (2013). Producing an Aristocracy of Culture in American Television. In G. R. Edgerton and J. P. Jones, eds., *The Essential HBO Reader*. Lexington: University Press of Kentucky, pp. 23–41.

Atherton, M. (2012). *There and Back Again: J. R. R. Tolkien and the Origins of* The Hobbit. London and New York: I. B. Tauris.

Babbage, Frances (2018). *Adaptation in Contemporary Theatre: Performing Literature*. London: Bloomsbury.

Bad Wolf (2018). Philip Pullman's *His Dark Materials*. https://bad-wolf.com/philip-pullmans-his-dark-materials-is-commissioned/.

Barnett, D. (2018). Making Fantasy Reality: Alan Lee, the Man Who Redrew Middle-Earth. *Guardian*, 3 September: www.theguardian.com/books/2018/sep/03/alan-lee-jrr-tolkien-the-lord-of-the-rings-the-hobbit-the-fall-of-gondolin.

Bauer, E. (2002). Peter Jackson. Creative *Screenwriting*, January–February: pp. 6–12.

Bellot, G. (2018). How Le Guin's *A Wizard of Earthsea* Subverts Racism (But Not Sexism). Tor.com, 30 October: www.tor.com/2018/10/30/how-le-guins-a-wizard-of-earthsea-subverts-racism-but-not-sexism/.

Berlatsky, N. (2015). Harry Potter and the Contradictions about Racial Justice. *Guardian*, 24 December: www.theguardian.com/books/2015/dec/24/harry-potter-race-muggles-black-hermione.

Billington, M. (2004). *His Dark Materials*. *Guardian*, 5 January: www.theguardian.com/stage/2004/jan/05/theatre.fiction.

Birns, N. (2018). *J. R. R. Tolkien: Architect of Modern Fantasy*. Farmington Hills, MI: Gale.

Blake, A. (2002). *The Irresistible Rise of Harry Potter*. London: Verso.

Bolter, J. D., and Grusin, R. (1999). *Remediation: Understanding New Media*. Cambridge: MIT Press.

Bourdaa, M. (2013). 'Following the Pattern': The Creation of an Encyclopaedic Universe with Transmedia Storytelling. *Adaptation*, 6 (2): pp. 202–14.

Bourdieu, P. (2002). The Field of Cultural Production. In D. Finkelstein and A. McCleery, eds., *The Book History Reader*. London and New York: Routledge.

Bristol, M. D. (2005). *Big-Time Shakespeare*. London and New York: Routledge.

Brown, M. (2014). George R. R. Martin: 'I Can Only Write One Word at a Time, One Book at a Time'. *Guardian*, 13 August: www.theguar dian.com/books/2014/aug/13/george-rr-martin-write-game-thrones-hbo.

Cain, R. (2017). Amazon's $250m *Lord of the Rings* Purchase Price Is 1,000 Times What Tolkien First Got for It. Forbes.com, 14 November: www.forbes.com/sites/robcain/2017/11/14/amazons-250m-lord-of-the-rings-purchase-price-is-1000-times-what-tolkien-first-got-for-it/#5d442c897273.

Carpenter, H., ed. (2006). *The Letters of J. R. R. Tolkien*. London: HarperCollins.

Carr, F. (2019). When Is the *Lord of the Rings* TV Series Released on Amazon? Who's in the Cast? What's It Going to Be About? *Radio Times*, 6 March: www.radiotimes.com/news/on-demand/2019–03-06/lord-of-the-rings-amazon-tv-series-release-date-cast-trailer-wri ters-prime-video/.

Chase, C. (1982). At the Movies: The Magic of Producing 'A Unicorn'. *New York Times*, 19 November: www.nytimes .com/1982/11/19/movies/at-the-movies-the-magic-of-produ cing-a-unicorn.html.

Child, B. (2015). Peter Jackson: 'I Didn't Know What the Hell I Was Doing' When I Made The Hobbit. *Guardian*, 19 November: www.theguardian.com/film/2015/nov/19/peter-jackson-battle-of-the-five-armies-i-didnt-know-what-the-hell-i-was-doing-when-i-made-the-hobbit.

Coleridge, S. T. (1834). *Biographia Literaria; Or, Biographical Sketches of My Literary Life and Opinions*. New York: Leavitt, Lord & Co.

Collins, J. (2010). *Bring on the Books for Everybody: How Literary Culture Became Popular Culture*. Durham, NC: Duke University Press.

Cooper, G. F. (2019). *Game of Thrones* Dragonmaster Reveals the Secrets of Daenerys' Babies. *Cnet.com*, 10 March: www.cnet.com/news/game-of-thrones-vfx-dragonmaster-reveals-secrets-of-daenerys-babies/.

Corriea, A. R. (2014). There and Back Again: A History of *The Lord of the Rings* in Video Games. *Polygon.com*, September: www.polygon.com/2014/9/23/6414775/lord-the-rings-tolkien-video-games.

Culhane, J. (1977). Will the Video Version of Tolkien Be Hobbit Forming? *New York Times*, 27 November: www.nytimes.com/1977/11/27/archives/will-the-video-version-of-tolkien-be-hobbit-forming.html.

Culhane, J. (1981). Ralph Bakshi: Iconoclast of Animation. *New York Times*, 22 March: www.nytimes.com/1981/03/22/arts/ralph-bakshi-iconoclast-of-animation.html.

Curry, P. (2004). *Defending Middle-Earth: Tolkien, Myth and Modernity*. New York: Houghton Mifflin.

Dargis, M. (2013). In the Middle of Middle Earth. *New York Times*, 12 December: www.nytimes.com/2013/12/13/movies/the-hobbit-the-desolation-of-smaug-with-ian-mckellen.html.

Day, J. (2001). Coke to Cash in on Harry Potter. *Guardian*, 20 February: www.theguardian.com/media/2001/feb/20/marketingandpr2.

Donaldson, S. (1986). *Epic Fantasy in the Modern World*. Kent, OH: Kent State University Library.

Donaldson, S. (2005, 2008). *Stephen R. Donaldson: The Official Website*: www.stephenrdonaldson.com/fromtheauthor/gi_view.php.

Dreyfuss, E. (2017). George R. R. Martin Doesn't Need to Finish Writing the *Game of Thrones* Books. *Wired.com*, 5 May: www.wired.com/2017/05/george-r-r-martin-game-of-thrones-books/.

Edwards, B. (2007). *C.S Lewis: Life, Works and Legacy*. Vol. 4.Westport, CN: Praeger.

Errington, P. W. (2017).*J. K. Rowling: A Bibliography*. London: Bloomsbury.

Eyre, C. (2014). Warner Bros. Creates Harry Potter Franchise Development Team. *TheBookseller.com*, 31 July: www.thebookseller.com/news/warner-bros-creates-harry-potter-franchise-development-team.

Fine, G. A. (1983). *Shared Fantasy: Role Playing Games as Social Worlds*. Chicago: University of Chicago Press.

Flood, A. (2018). George R. R .Martin: 'When I Began *A Game of Thrones* I Thought It Might Be a Short Story'. *Guardian*, 10 November: www.theguardian.com/books/2018/nov/10/books-interview-george-rr-martin.

Gekoski, R. (2004). *Tolkien's Gown & Other Stories of Great Authors and Rare Books*. London: Constable.

Genette, G. (1997). *Paratexts: Thresholds of Interpretation*. Trans. J. E. Lewin. Cambridge: Cambridge University Press.

Goff, P. (2006). Producing Harry Potter: Why the Medium Is Still the Message. In D. H. Nexon and I. B. Neumann, eds., *Harry Potter and International Relations*. New York: Rowman and Littlefield, pp. 27–44.

Goldstein, P., and Rainey, J. (2009). The Secret History of Why Disney Dumped 'Narnia'. *Los Angeles Times*, 19 January: https://latimes-blogs.latimes.com/the_big_picture/2009/01/the-secret-hist.html.

Grau, O. (2003). *Virtual Art: From Illusion to Immersion*. Cambridge: MIT Press.

Gray, J. (2010). *Show Sold Separately: Spoilers, Spinoffs, and Other Media Paratexts*. New York: New York University Press.

Greenway, J. (2019). Fans Are Ruining Game of Thrones – and Everything Else. *New Republic*, 21 May: https://newrepublic.com/article/153961/fans-ruining-game-thronesand-everything-else.

Groves, B. (2017). *Literary Allusion in Harry Potter*. London and New York: Routledge.

Grossman, L. (2011). George R. R. Martin's *Dance with Dragons*: A Masterpiece Worthy of Tolkien. *Time*, 7 July: http://content.time.com/time/arts/article/0,8599,2081774,00.html.

Gupta, S. (2009). *Re-Reading Harry Potter*. Houndmills, UK: Palgrave.

Hanel, M. (2012). From Sketch to Still: From Marbling Gringotts to Painting Diagon Alley, How Harry Potter's Art Direction Earned Its Oscar Nod. *Vanity Fair*, 14 February: www.vanityfair.com/culture/2012/02/harry-potter-exclusive-art-direction-room-of-require ment-special-effects.

Harmetz, A. (1978). Bakshi Journeys to Middle Earth to Animate 'Lord of the Rings'. *New York Times*, 8 November: www.nytimes.com/1978/11/08/archives/bakshi-journeys-to-middle-earth-to-animate-lord-of-the-rings-in.html.

Harris, C. (2001). *Dead until Dark*. New York: Ace Books.

Harvey, C., and Press, J. (1991). *William Morris: Design and Enterprise in Victorian Britain*. Manchester and New York: Manchester University Press.

Heritage, S. (2013). The Golden Compass Recap: How a Literary Triumph Was Turned to Dust. *Guardian*, 10 November: www.theguardian.com/film/2013/nov/10/golden-compass-film-recap.

Hibberd, J. (2016). *Game of Thrones*: Battle of the Bastards Director Speaks Out. *EW.com*, 9 June: https://ew.com/article/2016/06/19/game-thrones-battle-director/.

Hibberd, J. (2018). George R. R. Martin Gets Candid about New Book: 'What Excites Me Most Is I Finished It'. *Ew.com*, 19 November: https://ew.com/author-interviews/2018/11/19/george-rr-martin-interview/.

Hibberd, J. (2019). *Game of Thrones* First Look: Inside the Brutal Battle to Make Season 8. *EW.com*, 4 March: https://ew.com/tv/2019/03/04/game-of-thrones-season-8-battle/.

Hickey, W. (2015). Get Ready for Even More Off-Book *Game Of Thrones*. *Fivethirtyeight.com*, 15 June: https://fivethirtyeight.com/features/game-of-thrones-source-material-left-out/.

Hooton, C. (2018). The Long Night: *Game of Thrones* Prequel's 'Sociality' Could Take the Franchise Back to Its Roots. *Independent*, 31 October: www.independent.co.uk/arts-entertainment/tv/game-of-thrones/game-of-thrones-prequel-naomi-watts-the-long-night-spinoff-new-series-hbo-plot-news-a8610466.html.

Hutcheon, L. (2013). *A Theory of Adaptation*, 2nd ed. New York: Routledge.

Irwin, A. (2019). Shadows on the Wall. *Times Literary Supplement*, 7 June: pp. 20–1.

James, E. (2012). Tolkien, Lewis and the Explosion of Genre Fantasy. In E. James and F. Mendlesohn, eds., *The Cambridge Companion to Fantasy Literature*. Cambridge: Cambridge University Press, pp. 62–78.

Jenkins, H. (2006). *Convergence Culture: Where Old and New Media Collide*. New York: New York University Press.

Johnson, D. (2013). *Media Franchising: Creative License and Collaboration in the Culture Industries*. New York: New York University Press.

Kermode, M. (2014). *The Hobbit: The Battle of the Five Armies* Review – No More Than a Middling Finale from Middle-Earth. *Guardian*, 14 December: www.theguardian.com/film/2014/dec/14/the-hobbit-battle-five-armies-review-middling-finale-middle-earth.

Lanchester, J. (2019). You Win or You Die. *London Review of Books*, 6 June, p. 16.

Lanier, D. (2007). Shakespeare[TM]: Myth and Biographical Fiction. In R. Shaughnessy, ed., *The Cambridge Companion to Shakespeare and Popular Culture*. Cambridge: Cambridge University Press, pp. 93–113.

Latta, C. (2016). *C. S. Lewis and the Art of Writing*. Eugene: Cascade Books.

Le Guin, U. (2004). A Whitewashed Earthsea: How the Sci Fi Channel Wrecked My Books. *Slate.Com*, 16 December: https://slate.com/culture/2004/12/ursula-k-le-guin-on-the-tv-earthsea.html.

Lewis, C. S. (2012). *An Experiment in Criticism* (1961). Cambridge: Cambridge University Press.

Liptak, A. (2013). The Unauthorised Lord of the Rings. *Kirkusreviews.com*. 5 December: www.kirkusreviews.com/features/unauthorized-lord-rings/.

Lyman, R. (2001). Gambling on a Film Fantasy; 'Lord of the Rings' Shows New Line Cinema's Value to AOL. *New York Times*, 12 December: www.nytimes.com/2001/12/12/movies/gambling-film-fantasy-lord-rings-shows-new-line-cinema-s-value-aol.html.

Martin, G. R. R. (2014). *A Game of Thrones*. London: HarperCollins.

Matulef, J. (2011). *The Lord of the Rings: War in the North* Review. Eurogamer.com, 24 November: www.eurogamer.net/articles/2011-11-24-the-lord-of-the-rings-war-in-the-north-review.

McGrath, C. (2007). Unholy Production with a Fairy-tale Ending. *New York Times*, 2 December: www.nytimes.com/2007/12/02/movies/02mcgr.html.

Meikle, K. (2019). *Adaptations in the Franchise Era: 2001–16*. New York and London: Bloomsbury Academic.

Miller, L. (2005). Far from Narnia. *New Yorker*, 26 December: www.new yorker.com/magazine/2005/12/26/far-from-narnia.

Miller, M. (1999). 'Harry Potter' Casts a Spell Across the Ages. *Los Angeles Times*, 8 September: www.latimes.com/nation/la-na-potter-casts-spell-20170626-story.html.

Missingham, S. (2012). Interview: Charlie Redmayne, CEO of Pottermore. *TheBookseller.com*, 23 November: www.thebookseller.com/future book/interview-charlie-redmayne-ceo-pottermore.

Moher, A. (2018). Art of SFF: Charles Vess on Working with Ursula Le Guin on *The Books of Earthsea*. *Tor.com*, 9 November: www.tor.com/2018/11/09/art-of-sff-charles-vess-on-working-with-ursula-le-guin-on-the-books-of-earthsea/.

Murray, S. (2002). Harry Potter, Inc. Content Recycling for Corporate Synergy. *M/C Journal*, 5(4): http://journal.media-culture.org.au/0208/recycling.php.

Murray, S. (2012). *The Adaptation Industry: The Cultural Economy of Contemporary Literary Adaptation*. New York and London: Routledge.

Netflix Media Centre (2018). Netflix to Develop Series and Films Based on C. S. Lewis's Beloved *The Chronicles of Narnia*. *Netflix*, 3 October: https://media.netflix.com/en/press-releases/netflix-to-develop-series-and-films-based-on-c-s-lewis-beloved-the-chronicles-of-narnia.

O'Hehir, A. (2002). The Lord of the Rings: The Fellowship of the Ring. *Sight and Sound*, February, pp. 49–52.

Otterson, J. (2019). *Game of Thrones* Prequel Rounds Out Main Cast, S. J. Clarkson to Direct. *Variety.com*, 8 January: https://variety.com/2019/tv/news/game-of-thrones-prequel-cast-sj-clarkson-director-1203102426/.

Parker, L. (2014). A Gaming Company Devoted to Narrative Tackles *Thrones*. *New York Times*, 27 April: www.nytimes.com/192014/04/28/arts/video-games/a-gaming-company-devoted-to-narrative-tackles-thrones.html.

Parody, Clare (2011). Franchising/Adaptation. *Adaptation*, 4(2): pp. 210–18.

Paulson, M. (2018). Another Harry Potter Landmark: At $68 Million, the Most Expensive Broadway Nonmusical Play Ever. *New York Times*, 14 April: www.nytimes.com/2018/04/14/theater/harry-potter-broadway.html.

Perez, R. (2012). Peter Jackson Explains How 'The Lord of The Rings' Was Almost One Film Directed by John Madden and How Some Careful Lies Saved the Project in Four Weeks. *Indiewire.com*, 9 December: www.indiewire.com/2012/12/peter-jackson-explains-how-the-lord-of-the-rings-was-almost-one-film-directed-by-john-madden-how-some-careful-lies-saved-the-project-in-four-weeks–103140/.

Plesset, R. (2002). The Lord of the Rings: The Animated Films. *Cinefantastique*, 34(1): pp. 52–3.

Pottermore News Team (2018). 500 Million Harry Potter books Have Now Been Sold Worldwide. *Pottermore*, 1 February: https://www.pottermore.com/news/500-million-harry-potter-books-have-now-been-sold-worldwide.

Pullman, P. (1998). The Dark Side of Narnia. *Guardian*, 1 October, pp. 6–7.

Rankin, S. (2018). J. K. Rowling Answers EW's Burning Questions about *Fantastic Beasts: The Crimes of Grindelwald. EW.com*, 16 October: https://ew.com/movies/2018/10/16/jk-rowling-interview-fantastic-beasts-crimes-grindelwald/.

Rapold, N. (2014). Bilbo Baggins in the Shadow of Bloodthirsty Hordes. *New York Times*, 16 December: www.nytimes.com/2014/12/17/movies/the-hobbit-the-battle-of-the-five-armies.html.

Ravindran, M. (2018). Netflix Sets Out for Narnia with eOne's Mark Gordon. *TBIVision*, 4 October: https://tbivision.com/2018/10/04/netflix-sets-out-for-narnia-with-eones-mark-gordon/.

Renfro, K. (2017). Inside the New Battle-Ready Looks of the *Game of Thrones* Queens. *ThisIsInsider.com*, 28 June: www.thisisinsider.com/game-of-thrones-costume-designer-michele-clapton-interview–2017–6.

Rich, M. (2007a). The Voice of Harry Potter Can Keep a Secret. *New York Times*, 17 July: www.nytimes.com/2007/07/17/books/17dale.html.

Rich, M. (2007b). Record First-Day Sales for Last 'Harry Potter' Book. *New York Times*, 22 July: www.nytimes.com/2007/07/22/books/22cnd-potter.html.

Riley, A. (2010). Sucking the Quileute Dry. *New York Times*, 7 February: www.nytimes.com/2010/02/08/opinion/08riley.html.

Rissik, A. (2000). Middle-Earth, Middlebrow. *Guardian*, 2 September: www.theguardian.com/books/2000/sep/02/jrrtolkien.classics.

Robinson, J. (2017). *Game of Thrones*: The Final Season Has an Insanely Huge Budget. *Vanity Fair*, 26 September: www.vanityfair.com/hollywood/2017/09/game-of-thrones-how-much-does-the-final-season-8-cost-per-episode-15-million.

Robinson, J. (2018). *Game of Thrones*: The Secrets of George R. R. Martin's Final Script. *Vanity Fair*, 7 December: www.vanityfair.com/hollywood/2018/12/game-of-thrones-george-rr-martin-last-script-the-lion-and-the-rose.

Rowling, J. K. (2001). *Fantastic Beasts and Where to Find Them*. London: Bloomsbury.

Rowling, J. K. (2013). *Harry Potter and the Philosopher's Stone*. London: Bloomsbury.

Rubin, R. L. (2012). *Well Met: Renaissance Fairies and the American Counterculture*. New York and London: New York University Press.

Salen, K., and Zimmerman, E. (2004). *Rules of Play: Game Design Fundamentals*. Cambridge: MIT Press.

Saler, M. (2012). *As If: Modern Enchantment and the Literary Prehistory of Virtual Reality*. Oxford: Oxford University Press.

Saraiya, S. (2014). The Violent Wonderland of *Game of Thrones*. *TV.avclub.com*, 13 June: https://tv.avclub.com/the-violent-wonderland-of-game-of-thrones–1798269407.

Saraiya, S. (2016). *Game of Thrones* Goes to War: The Once-Radical Fantasy Is Now the Establishment – For Better and for Worse. *Salon.com*, 24 April: www.salon.com/2016/04/24/game_of_thrones_goes_to_war_the_once_radical_fantasy_is_now_the_establishment_for_better_and_for_worse/.

Scott, A. O. (2012). Bilbo Begins His Ring Cycle. *New York Times*. 13 December: www.nytimes.com/2012/12/14/movies/the-hobbit-an-unexpected-journey-by-peter-jackson.html.

Seale, J. (2015). George R. R. Martin: Hollywood Would Have Ruined *Game of Thrones*. *Guardian*, 10 June: www.theguardian.com/tv-and-radio/tvandradioblog/2015/jun/10/george-rr-martin-hollywood-would-have-ruined-game-of-thrones.

Shamsian, J. (2018). The Woman Who Illustrated 'Harry Potter' Barely Spoke to J. K. Rowling while She Completed All 7 Books. *ThisIsInsider.com*, 13 November: www.thisisinsider.com/mary-grandpre-jk-rowling-book-illustrations-relationship-2018-11.

Sharf, Z. (2018). Catherine Hardwicke Fought for 'Twilight' to Feature Diverse Cast, but Stephenie Meyer Rejected Her Idea. *Indiewire.com*, 3 October: www.indiewire.com/2018/10/catherine-hardwicke-twilight-diverse-cast-stephenie-meyer-refused–1202009330/.

Shippey, T. (2000). *J. R. R. Tolkien: Author of the Century*. London: HarperCollins.

Shippey, T. (2003). From Page to Screen: J. R. R. Tolkien and Peter Jackson. *World Literature Today*. 77(2): pp. 69–72.

Sibley, B. (2008). 'Pauline Baynes: Illustrator Who Depicted Lewis's Narnia and Tolkien's Middle-Earth'. *Independent*, 6 August: www.independent.co.uk/news/obituaries/pauline-baynes-illustrator-who-depicted-lewiss-narnia-and-tolkiens-middle-earth-886121.html.

Siede, C. (2016). *Game of Thrones* Has Ushered in the Golden Age of Internet Fandom. *QZ.com*, 7 June: https://qz.com/699381/game-of-thrones-has-ushered-in-the-golden-age-of-internet-fandom/.

Siegel, T. (2014). Multiples *Game of Thrones* Movies Eyes by George R. R. Martin. *Hollywoodreporter.com*, 19 March: www.hollywoodreporter.com/heat-vision/game-thrones-movies-eyed-by–689629.

Smith, A. (2018). *Storytelling Industries: Narrative Production in the 21ˢᵗ Century*. Basingstoke, UK: Palgrave.

Smith, D. (2000). The *Times* Plans a Children's Best-Seller List. *New York Times*, 24 June: www.nytimes.com/2000/06/24/books/the-times-plans-a-children-s-best-seller-list.html?.

Stamp, E. (2011). Inside *Harry Potter and the Deathly Hallows: Part 2*. *ArchitecturalDigest.com*, 1 July: www.architecturaldigest.com/story/harry-potter-set-design-article.

Steafel, E. (2016). I Told J K Rowling She'd Never Make Any Money from Harry Potter. *Telegraph*, 10 December: www.telegraph.co.uk/men/thinking-man/told-j-k-rowling-never-make-money-harry-potter/.

Takanashi, D. (2017). Middle-Earth: Shadow of War Post-Mortem – Monolith's Michael De Plater Explains It All. *Venturebeat.com*, 17 October: https://venturebeat.com/2017/10/17/game-boss-interview-michael-de-platers-postmortem-on-middle-earth-shadow-of-war/.

Tassi, P. (2018). *Game of Thrones* Showrunners Doing *Star Wars* Is Worrisome for a Few Reasons. *Forbes*, 7 February: www.forbes .com/sites/insertcoin/2018/02/07/game-of-thrones-showrunners-doing-star-wars-is-worrisome-for-a-few-reasons/#67504d844d0e.

Taylor, G. (2017). Artiginality: Authorship after Postmodernism. In G. Taylor and G. Egan, eds., *The New Oxford Shakespeare: Authorship Companion*. Oxford: Oxford University Press, pp. 3–26.

Thompson, E. P. (2011). *William Morris: Romantic to Revolutionary*. Oakland: PM Press and Merlin Press.

Thompson, K. (2007). *The Frodo Franchise: The Lord of the Rings and Modern Hollywood*. Berkeley: University of California Press.

Tolkien, J. R. R. (2001). On Fairy Stories. In *Tree and Leaf*. London: HarperCollins.

Toynbee, P. (2005). Narnia Represents Everything That Is Most Hateful about Religion. *Guardian*, 5 December: www.theguardian.com/ books/2005/dec/05/cslewis.booksforchildrenandteenagers.

Trueman, M. (2012). Narnia – The Next Stage Spectacular. *Guardian*, 3 January: www.theguardian.com/stage/2012/jan/03/narnia-the-next-stage-spectacular.

Turner. J. (2001). Reasons for Liking Tolkien. *London Review of Books*, 23 (22): www.lrb.co.uk/v23/n22/jenny-turner/reasons-for-liking-tolkien.

Voigts-Virchow, E. (2017). Anti-essentialist Versions of Aggregate Alice: A Grin without a Cat. In K. Krebs, ed., *Translation and Adaptation in Theatre and Film*. London and New York: Routledge, pp. 63–79.

Wahlquist, C. (2019). The *Cursed Child* in Australia: It's Harry Potter for People Who Never Really Liked Him. *Guardian*, 23 February: www.theguardian.com/stage/2019/feb/24/the-cursed-child-in-aus tralia-its-harry-potter-for-people-who-never-really-liked-him.

Wasko, J., and Shanadi, G. (2006). More Than Just Rings: Merchandise for Them All. In E. Mathijs, ed., *The Lord of the Rings: Popular Culture in Global Context*. New York: Wallflower Press, pp. 23–42.

Whitehead, A. (2018). Sales of *A Song of Ice and Fire* Overtake *The Wheel of Time* and *DiscWorld*. *The WertZone: SF in Print and On Screen*, 28 July: http://thewertzone.blogspot.com/2018/07/sales-of-song-of-ice-and-fire-overtake.html.

Wilkin, S. (2012). 'Harry Potter' Studio Tour Interview: Nick Dudman Talks Designing Magical Creatures. *Hypable.com*, 1 April: www.hypable.com/harry-potter-studio-tour-interview-nick-dudman-talks-designing-magical-creatures/.

Williams, S. (2012). *The Lion, the Witch and the Wardrobe*: Narnia in the Park. *Telegraph*, 29 May: www.telegraph.co.uk/culture/theatre/theatre-features/9284983/Lion-the-Witch-and-the-Wardrobe-Narnia-in-the-park.html.

Windolf, J. (2014). The Gathering Storm. *Vanity Fair*, April: www.vanityfair.com/hollywood/2014/04/game-of-thrones-season–4.

Wright, E.B. (2010). Creating Dothraki: An Interview with David J. Peterson and Sai Emrys. *Tor.com*, 22 April: www.tor.com/2010/04/22/creating-dothraki-an-interview-with-david-j-peterson-and-sai-emrys/.

Yu, C. (2018). George R. R. Martin, Fantasy's Reigning King. *New York Times Style Magazine*, 15 October: www.nytimes.com/2018/10/15/t-magazine/george-rr-martin-got-interview.html.

Cambridge Elements ≡

Publishing and Book Culture

SERIES EDITOR

Samantha Rayner
University College London

Samantha Rayner is a reader in University College London's
(UCL's) Department of Information Studies. She is also
director of UCL's Centre for Publishing, co-director of the
Bloomsbury CHAPTER (Communication History,
Authorship, Publishing, Textual Editing and Reading) and co-
editor of the Academic Book of the Future BOOC (Book as
Open Online Content) with UCL Press.

ASSOCIATE EDITOR

Rebecca Lyons
University of Bristol

Rebecca Lyons is a teaching fellow at the University of Bristol.
She is also co-editor of the experimental BOOC (Book as Open
Online Content) at UCL Press. She teaches and researches book
and reading history, particularly female owners and readers of
Arthurian literature in fifteenth- and sixteenth-century England,
and also has research interests in digital academic publishing.

About the Series

This series aims to fill the demand for easily accessible, quality texts available for teaching and research in the diverse and dynamic fields of Publishing and Book Culture. Rigorously researched and peer-reviewed Elements will be published under themes, or 'Gatherings'. These Elements should be the first checkpoint for researchers or students working on that area of publishing and book trade history and practice: we hope that, situated so logically at Cambridge University Press, where academic publishing in the United Kingdom began, it will create an unrivalled space where these histories and practices can be investigated and preserved.

Cambridge Elements ⹀

Publishing and Book Culture
Bestsellers

Gathering Editor: Beth Driscoll
Beth Driscoll is Senior Lecturer in Publishing and Communications
at the University of Melbourne. She is the author of *The New Literary
Middlebrow* (Palgrave Macmillan, 2014), and her research interests
include contemporary reading and publishing, genre fiction and
post-digital literary culture.

Gathering Editor: Lisa Fletcher
Lisa Fletcher is Associate Professor of English at the University of
Tasmania. Her books include *Historical Romance Fiction:
Heterosexuality and Performativity* (Ashgate, 2008) and *Popular
Fiction and Spatiality: Reading Genre Settings* (Palgrave Macmillan,
2016).

Gathering Editor: Kim Wilkins
Kim Wilkins is an Associate Professor of Writing and Publishing at
the University of Queensland. She is also the author of more than
thirty popular fiction novels.

ELEMENTS IN THE GATHERING

Adapting Bestsellers: Fantasy, Franchise and the Afterlife of Storyworlds
Ken Gelder

A full series listing is available at: www.cambridge.org/EPBC

Printed in the United States
By Bookmasters